BBC MUSIC GUIDES

———

FALLA

BBC MUSIC GUIDES

Bach Cantatas J. A. WESTRUP
Bach Organ Music PETER WILLIAMS
Bartók Chamber Music STEPHEN WALSH
Bartók Orchestral Music JOHN MCCABE
Beethoven Concertos and Overtures ROGER FISKE
Beethoven Piano Sonatas DENIS MATTHEWS
Beethoven String Quartets BASIL LAM
Beethoven Symphonies ROBERT SIMPSON
Berlioz Orchestral Music HUGH MACDONALD
Brahms Chamber Music IVOR KEYS
Brahms Piano Music DENIS MATTHEWS
Brahms Orchestral Music JOHN HORTON
Brahms Songs ERIC SAMS
Bruckner Symphonies PHILIP BARFORD
Couperin DAVID TUNLEY
Debussy Orchestral Music DAVID COX
Debussy Piano Music FRANK DAWES
Dvořák Symphonies and Concertos ROBERT LAYTON
Elgar Orchestral Music MICHAEL KENNEDY
Handel Concertos STANLEY SADIE
Haydn String Quartets ROSEMARY HUGHES
Haydn Symphonies H. C. ROBBINS LANDON
Mahler Symphonies and Songs PHILIP BARFORD
Mendelssohn Chamber Music JOHN HORTON
Monteverdi Church Music DENIS ARNOLD
Monteverdi Madrigals DENIS ARNOLD
Mozart Chamber Music A. HYATT KING
Mozart Piano Concertos PHILIP RADCLIFFE
Mozart Serenades, Divertimenti and Dances ERIK SMITH
Mozart Wind and String Concertos A. HYATT KING
Purcell ARTHUR HUTCHINGS
Rachmaninov Orchestral Music PATRICK PIGGOTT
Ravel Orchestral Music LAURENCE DAVIES
Schoenberg Chamber Music ARNOLD WHITTALL
Schubert Chamber Music J. A. WESTRUP
Schubert Piano Sonatas PHILIP RADCLIFFE
Schubert Songs MAURICE J. E. BROWN
Schubert Symphonies MAURICE J. E. BROWN
Schumann Orchestral Music HANS GAL
Schumann Piano Music JOAN CHISSELL
Schumann Songs ASTRA DESMOND
Shostakovich Symphonies HUGH OTTAWAY
Tchaikovsky Ballet Music JOHN WARRACK
Tchaikovsky Symphonies and Concertos JOHN WARRACK
The Trio Sonata CHRISTOPHER HOGWOOD
Vaughan Williams Symphonies HUGH OTTAWAY
Vivaldi MICHAEL TALBOT
Hugo Wolf Songs MOSCO CARNER

BBC MUSIC GUIDES

Falla

RONALD CRICHTON

BRITISH BROADCASTING CORPORATION

The music examples are reproduced by
kind permission of J. & W. Chester/
Edition Wilhelm Hansen London Ltd;
Max Eschig, Paris; Durand, Paris;
and Ricordi, Milan.

Published by the
British Broadcasting Corporation
35 Marylebone High Street
London W1M 4AA

ISBN 0 563 17820 5

First published 1982

© Ronald Crichton 1982

Filmset in Great Britain by
August Filmsetting, Warrington, Cheshire
Printed in England by Hollen Street Press, Slough, Bucks

Contents

Acknowledgements	6
Introduction	7
Cadiz and Madrid, 1876–1907	9
Paris, 1907–14	16
Madrid Again, 1914–20	25
Granada, 1920–39	49
Argentina, 1939–46	76
Style and Man	95
Index of Works	104

Acknowledgements

I am indebted to María Isabel de Falla and her husband, José María García de Paredes, for their unfailingly generous and helpful co-operation. Angel Sagardía enabled me to see rare material in his possession. Juan Soriano gave invaluable assistance in Barcelona and London. Thanks are due to the BBC Music Library, the Science Reference Library, Westminster City Libraries and the British Institute of Recorded Sound in London, to the National Library of Scotland in Edinburgh, to the Biblioteca de Catalunya and Biblioteca del Orfeó Català in Barcelona. Messrs G. Ricordi & Co. (Milan and London) provided information about *Atlántida* and gave permission to quote from *Musica d'oggi*. Messrs J. & W. Chester Ltd and the English Bach Festival Trust in London have allowed the re-use of material that appeared in more or less similar form in my *Descriptive Catalogue* and in EBF programme-books. Permission to reproduce music examples was given by: Chester Music (*El amor brujo*, *The Three-Cornered Hat*, *Fantasía baetica*, *Master Peter's Puppet Show*, *Homenaje 'Le Tombeau de Claude Debussy'*); Durand et Cie (*Pièces espagnoles*, Debussy, *Préludes pour piano, 1er livre*); Max Eschig (*La vida breve*, *Seven Spanish Folksongs*, *Nights in the Gardens of Spain*, *Concerto*); Hamelle (d'Indy, *Symphonie cévenole*); Ricordi (*Balada de Mallorca*, *Atlántida*).

Introduction

Falla was the outstanding Spanish composer of modern times and one of the leading European composers of the first half of the present century. Nevertheless, from the outbreak of the Civil War in 1936 until quite recently, and except for brief bursts of interest caused by the successive premières of *Atlántida*, his position was paradoxical. The popularity of his music rested on a few works (or excerpts from works) out of a total output small enough in all conscience. Otherwise he became a largely unknown, even inaccessible figure. There were reasons for this apart from the usual ups and downs of reputation and shifts of taste that follow the death of a creative artist – and for many music-lovers outside Spanish-speaking lands Falla virtually died in 1936, ten years before his actual death. The Falla papers, cared for after his death by his brother and then by his niece and her husband, were not easily available for inspection during the years of Spain's cultural quasi-isolation. The new régime in Spain after the death of General Franco and the centenary of Falla's birth in 1976 caused a revival of interest in his work as a whole, suitably marked by the construction at Granada of a fine new building on the hill behind his former home. The Centro 'Manuel de Falla', opened in 1977, comprises concert and exhibition halls with space as well for summer schools, master classes and the housing and study of archive material.

Under the circumstances it is hardly surprising that while there are plenty of books about Falla there is so far no definitive biography. The gap needs filling. The number of people who knew him well during the Granada period or the final years in remote Argentina are fast decreasing. Aspects of his personal life remain obscure. What was the exact nature of the illnesses that afflicted him from early middle age onwards? To what extent were they responsible for the slow genesis and non-completion of *Atlántida*? There is another reason for wanting to know more. Falla was an intensely private man, yet he played his role as a public figure conscientiously both in Spain and abroad. His comings and goings, meetings and friendships with a wide range of notable musicians (and, in Spain, with writers and painters) deserve full documentation. Although his voluminous correspondence has been drawn upon and quoted by biographers, only a portion (notably the letters to the Sevillian cellist, Segismundo Romero) has been published.

Falla was a ready letter-writer (sometimes when he was ill, his sister María del Carmen wrote in his place: her formal near-copperplate is in striking contrast to her brother's nervous, hurried, not always easily decipherable hand), addicted also to the use of picture-postcards of the old sepia type, on which he contrived to insert a surprising amount of information. He was not a man to unburden himself, but to close friends he wrote freely, and when he was at home in Granada he was hungry for news of people and events nearer the centre of the musical world – for Falla not Germany or Austria so much as Paris, Italy or even England (during his life-time, most of his music was published in Paris or London).

Little has appeared about him in England since J. B. Trend's still useful *Manuel de Falla and Spanish Music* (New York and London, 1929, reprinted 1935). Two general surveys, published or obtain-able here, containing material on Falla are Gilbert Chase's *The Music of Spain* (New York, 1941, paperback edition, revised and enlarged, 1959) and Ann Livermore's *Short History of Spanish Music* (London, 1972). Falla's collected writings, with the original intro-duction and notes by F. Sopeña, have been translated by David Urman and J. M. Thomson as *Manuel de Falla on Music and Musicians* (London, 1979). Burnett James's *Manuel de Falla and the Spanish Musical Renaissance* (London, 1979) sets Falla's achievement against the national background. The present writer's *Manuel de Falla: Descriptive Catalogue of his works* (London, 1976) provides fuller performance details, lists, etc., than is possible here. Kenneth Thompson's *A Dictionary of Twentieth-Century Composers* (London, 1973) contains a detailed bibliography of Falla. Vol. 6 of the *New Grove Dictionary of Music and Musicians* (London, 1980) includes a comprehensive entry on Falla, with work list, by Enrique Franco.

In France, Roland-Manuel's monograph *Manuel de Falla* (Paris, 1930, reissued 1977) remains the most perceptive single piece of writing about Falla. The most comprehensive, balanced, clearly arranged study is *Manuel de Falla* by Suzanne Demarquez (Paris, 1963, English trans. USA and Canada, 1968, Spanish trans. Bar-celona, 1968). Luis Campodonico's *Falla*, translated into French from the Spanish (Paris, 1959) is stimulating.

For Spanish readers the field is wider, including among other books Jaime Pahissa's *Vida y obra de Manuel de Falla* (Buenos Aires, 1956, English trans. from an earlier edition, London, 1954), Federico Sopeña's *Atlántida: Introducción a Manuel de Falla* (Madrid,

1962), Angel Sagardía's *Vida y obra de Manuel de Falla* (Madrid, 1967), Manuel Orozco's copiously illustrated *Falla* (Barcelona, 1968), and Falla's writings, collected under the title *Escritos sobre música y músicos*, ed. F. Sopeña (Madrid, 1950, 3rd augmented ed. 1972). The letters referred to earlier are contained in Manuel de Falla: *Cartas a Segismundo Romero*, ed. and introduced by Pascual Pascual Recuero (Granada, 1976). In a class by itself stands the discursive, detailed study of Falla during his two visits to Majorca by his cicerone Juan María Thomas: *Manuel de Falla en la isla* (Mallorca, 1947). Important articles in Italian and Spanish periodicals are mentioned in the text. In his *Cien artículos* (Madrid, 1957), José María Pemán included personal reminiscences of Falla much quoted by other writers. Less well known is a chapter of recollections of Falla in Barcelona in María Martínez Sierra's *Gregorio y yo* (Mexico City, 1953). A special Falla centenary number (592–3) of the periodical *La estafeta literaria* (Madrid, 1976) contains a useful bibliography by José Blas Vega. Francisco García Lorca's study of his brother, *Federico y su mundo* (Madrid, 1980), includes a section on Falla and Lorca.

The first five sections of what follows reflect convenient divisions in Falla's life. In each case a biographical summary precedes discussion of the music produced during the years in question. The music is not always taken in exact chronological order. For example, while *La vida breve* was written during the first Madrid period, the finishing touches were given and the first productions took place in France. The opera is therefore included in the 'Paris' section. It seemed preferable to discuss the two ballets in succession, although the first performance of *Nights in the Gardens of Spain* came in between. The four *Homenajes*, although their composition was spread over nearly the whole of Falla's Granada period, are treated together as they occur in the orchestral version of 1939. *Atlántida*, begun in the Granada years, is described (as befits Falla's last, unfinished work) in the fifth, 'Argentina', section.

Cadiz and Madrid, 1876–1907

Cadiz projects like a swollen sickle into the sea near the southernmost point of Spain. In ancient times it was on the rim of the world.

When navigators sailed over that rim, Cadiz became a gateway to the New World. The situation was strategic: a few miles to the East, at Tarifa, where you can see the mountains of Morocco across the Straits, the waters of the Mediterranean mingle with the Atlantic. Except that the narrow isthmus joining Cadiz to the mainland is now clustered with high-rise buildings, the old city, with paved streets, tightly-packed white houses with glazed balconies and doors of stout mahogany studded with brass, gardens overlooking the sea and a vast baroque cathedral, must look much the same as it did when Manuel María de los Dolores de Falla y Matheu was born there on 23 November 1876.

Neither of his parents was of old Andalusian stock. The father was a businessman of Valencian descent, the mother, María del Carmen Matheu Asturias, was Catalan, a fact worth mentioning since Spanish regionalism was to play a part in Falla's music. Commercial activity made Cadiz more cosmopolitan in temper than many Andalusian cities, though such distinctions would have been lost on the dreamy, withdrawn child Manuel became. (Of five children, three survived: Manuel, a younger brother Germán, and a sister, María del Carmen.) Manuel invented for himself an imaginary city called Colón (he may have been stimulated by a visit to Seville, to which he took a violent liking), working out the details with elaborate care – they included newspapers, an opera house, even an opera. The family doctor put an end to the fantasy but did not discourage a passion for toy theatres. Though his parents gave him a ready-made one, he preferred another made by himself with puppets worked by his brother and sister.

Musical life in Cadiz was provincial but not ignobly so. There was one unique feature, the annual Good Friday performance of Haydn's *The Seven Words of the Saviour on the Cross*, commissioned by a canon of the cathedral while Haydn was working at Eszterháza. There were occasional opera seasons and public concerts as well as music-making in the home, ranging from salon music and excerpts from (and fantasias on) familiar operas to occasional chamber music. Beyond this was something that cities outside the province could not boast – the wealth of Andalusian folk music still performed not as a self-conscious survival but as a natural, deliberate way of life, likely to make a permanent impression on a sensitive, intelligent child.

Falla's mother gave him his first music lessons, but his ambitions were more literary than musical until 1893, when an orchestra was formed to give concerts in the city picture gallery, against a background of smouldering canvases by Zurbarán. Now the pendulum swung the other way, and Falla began to take advanced piano lessons and to study harmony and counterpoint. There were enthusiastic and knowledgeable music lovers to encourage and guide him, such as Salvador Viniegra, amateur cellist, lover of Wagner's music and friend of Saint-Saëns, who used to stay with Viniegra on his way to the Canaries; and Manuel Quirell, who ran a music shop, with a recital room, in the town. Falla's childhood marked him deeply and his love for his birthplace never weakened. The years in Cadiz, moreover, were a time of material comfort which never returned.

Towards the end of the century the family fortunes declined. In 1896 they moved to Madrid, where Manuel had already been going for lessons with a piano teacher of some renown, José Tragó. Now he joined the Conservatoire, continued his lessons with Tragó and went through the seven-year course in the space of two years, winning the first prize. Links with Cadiz were not severed. He returned there to see friends and to give private and public concerts at which some of his early efforts were performed. Though his talent, as pianist if not yet as composer, was clearly established, it was a fairly late flowering. Falla was neither precocious nor a prodigy. By the time of the move to Madrid he was twenty.

Madrid offered more than distant Cadiz, but musical life there was still provincialism, only writ larger. The situation in Spain towards the end of the century had something in common with that in England. In both, foreign styles were rampant, Italian and French stronger in Spain, German in England. In both countries the surest signs of vitality lay in light opera – Sullivan in England, the zarzuela composers in Spain. There were, national temperaments and life-styles apart, two main differences. In Spain there was nothing comparable to the Protestant oratorio tradition of England – however comatose church music had become since Mendelssohn, the tradition still offered a living to composers and performers. The British Isles, on the other hand, having passed through the Industrial Revolution, were fast losing their folk music as rural life was changed by the rapid growth of towns. Our collectors were just in time. In Spain the great diversity of folk music was still a living tradition, possibly not so secure as it seemed, but not in danger of extinction. The two sides of the picture are connected. The backward conditions which in Spain ensured the survival of so much traditional song and dance did little or nothing to help the cultivation of music at more sophisticated levels. Britain unindustrialised would hardly have possessed such choral and orchestral resources as had developed outside London during the nineteenth century. In both countries, grand as opposed to light opera was a seasonal business, concerned where possible with star singers.

Family prosperity having gone, Falla had to earn his living. He emerged from his studies at the Conservatoire as a virtuoso pianist of promise with a small sheaf of compositions and few prospects except for occasional engagements as a pianist and the usual chores, such as accompanying and teaching. A musical backwater Madrid may have been, but news from the outer world seeped through, and Falla was aware of what was going on in Paris. The French capital became the Promised Land: he was determined to get there. Meanwhile, in order to live, he had like many other composers with high ambitions to write *zarzuelas*.

The *zarzuela* of Falla's day was an operetta in one or more acts (many of the most popular are one-acters), genre pieces in the musical and linguistic vernacular, often with urban or metropolitan settings. There was nothing inherently disreputable in the genre. Many composers of famous examples like Barbieri (*Pan y toros, El barberillo de Lavapiés*), Bretón (*La verbena de la Paloma*) and Vives (*Doña Francisquita*) were versatile and respected musicians. Barbieri, for example, had been a pioneer musicologist, Bretón was head of the Madrid Conservatoire when Falla was a student there. But *zarzuelas* were not what Falla wanted to write. Nevertheless he produced five, two of them in collaboration with a successful practitioner, Amadeo Vives, three on his own. Falla's were not successful and only one, *Los amores de la Inés*, reached the stage. Two things, however, happened to him in these years which had greater effect on the development of his music than the writing of *zarzuelas*, and brought to an end the period which the writer Gerardo Diego referred to as 'Premanuel de Antefalla'.

The first event was the publication in the *Revista musical catalan* of a page from Pedrell's opera *Los Pirineos*,[1] given in Barcelona in

[1] This opera is often referred to as a 'trilogy', a designation which produces some confusion. *Los Pirineos*, in a prologue and three acts, is indeed described on the title-page as a 'trilogia': it also forms the first part of a

1902. The extract had a revelatory effect on Falla, who had met Pedrell but did not know his music. Viniegra gave him a letter of introduction. Felipe Pedrell (1841–1922), composer, pedagogue, folksong collector, researcher and editor, was then living and teaching in Madrid. Falla arrived to find the older man in unreceptive mood, unwilling to take more pupils, but relenting in the face of Falla's sincerity and determination. In the two years or so that remained before he returned to Barcelona, Pedrell put Falla on his true path, introducing him to the polyphonic music of Spain's great centuries, to the wealth of folk music, much of it quite different from the Andalusian kind Falla grew up with, also guiding him through recent musical developments, especially those in Russia and France. For Falla, Pedrell was the right man at the right moment, monumentally erudite, a teacher of high ideals who was at the same time sensible and practical – he did not discourage the modest work Falla was doing (he had written *zarzuelas* himself many years ago), but helped him. Falla for his part had the temperament and disposition to profit from Pedrell's guidance as some earlier pupils, even when they were as gifted as Albéniz and Granados, had not. Pedrell was the greatest influence on Falla's development as a composer apart from Debussy and the other brilliant musicians he came to know in Paris. Without his formative influence, Falla would have been less fitted to profit from his experiences in Paris.

The second event was the chance discovery in 1906 on a second-hand bookstall in a Madrid street of a small volume, *L'Acoustique nouvelle*, by the French writer Louis Lucas (see p. 97).

In 1904 two competitions were announced. The first, organised by the Royal Academy of San Fernando, was for various types of composition including one-act operas and symphonic works – symphonic music, like grand opera, being in an ailing condition. The second, sponsored by the Madrid piano makers Ortiz y Cussó, offered pianists one of their instruments as a prize. Falla, scenting a possible means of getting to Paris, decided to enter for the opera competition. His teacher Tragó persuaded him to try for the piano prize as well. Inconveniently from the point of view of anyone wanting to enter for both, the piano contest was to be held on the day after the last date for submission of the opera scores.

For his one-act opera, *La vida breve*, Falla chose a text by an larger Fatherland–Love–Faith trilogy embracing two other large works, *La Celestina* (Love) and *El Comte Arnau* (Faith).

13

acquaintance from Cadiz, Carlos Fernández Shaw, an experienced writer of *zarzuela* libretti. According to the author's son Guillermo, whose book *Larga historia de 'La vida breve'*, published in 1972, differs in some respects from previous accounts, the choice had been made and work started on the opera before the competiton was announced. Even so, Falla only just finished the score on time. On the following day he won the piano contest, the runner-up being Frank Marshall, a distinguished Granados pupil from Barcelona who became a close friend. At this stage and for some years after, Falla was capable of such sustained feats of physical and mental energy. They may, all the same, have contributed to the decline in health to which his slight physique was before long to be subjected.

In due course Falla was named as the winner of the opera competition. All seemed well, but the rules included a rather vaguely phrased clause appearing to guarantee a production in Madrid of the winning opera. In fact the Academy of San Fernando had no means of compelling the Royal Theatre (leased to an impresario who was unlikely to take risks with untried modern works) or anyone else to stage *La vida breve*. They could only hope for co-operation. There followed a time of mortification and frustration for Falla, who was counting on the money the opera should have brought him to get to Paris. The eventual means of escape was a job as pianist to a mime troupe performing Wormser's once popular pantomime *L'Enfant prodigue* on a tour through France, Belgium, Switzerland and parts of Germany. Finally he found himself on his own in Paris.

EARLY WORKS

Published

Piano solo: *Vals-capricho* (Valse caprice); *Serenata andaluza*; *Nocturno*; *Danza de gnomos*; *Canción*.

Voice and piano: *Tus ojillos negros* (Your little black eyes) – words by Cristóbal de Castro; *Preludios* (words by Antonio de Trueba); *Olas gigantes* and *Dios mio, que solos* – both with words from the *Rimas* of Gustavo Adolfo Bécquer.

Violoncello and piano: *Melodía*; *Romanza*.

Nocturno and *Serenata andaluza*, salon pieces with Spanish colouring, were played by Falla at Cadiz in September 1899 and September 1900 respectively. Exact dates of composition are uncertain. *Vals-*

capricho, with a café-chantant tune and a whiff of Chabrier in the harmony, is more interesting. The song, *Tus ojillos negros*, has an impulsive first idea over flowing quaver accompaniment. The piano pieces, *Nocturno* excepted, and the song were published by Faustino Fuente of Madrid. No copyright was taken out. They were re-published without authorisation in the USA. Finally Union Musical Española republished them, with *Nocturno*, in 1940 in Madrid. The remaining piano pieces and songs, and the cello pieces, had to wait until 1980 for publication (by the same firm) as *Obras desconocidas* (3 vols). *Danza de gnomos* (Gnomes' dance) is a simple, Griegian piece of some charm. The melancholy *Canción* might almost be mistaken for a lost *Gymnopédie* of Satie. The songs already show Falla's feeling for vocal lines. The first of the two Bécquer settings, *Olas gigantes*, is a stormy, effective essay in the line of Schumann and Grieg. The piano parts of the other songs are conventional. The cello pieces, written for Viniegra, were performed by him and by Falla at Cadiz in 1897 (the *Melodía* was the composer's first acknowledged work) and 1899 respectively. Both are in the elegiac mood of Massenet or early Fauré.

Los amores de la Inés

The only one of Falla's *zarzuelas* to reach the stage (Teatro Cómico, Madrid, 1902) is a 'sainete lirico' in one act with libretto by Emilio Dugi or Duggi. There are a Prelude and five numbers including an orchestral intermezzo. Of the vocal numbers only the third, a duet for soprano and tenor in the alternating 3/4 and 6/8 Falla was to handle so well in, eg, 'Cubana' from the *Pièces espagnoles*, is of interest. A vocal score was published in 1965 by Union Musical Española, Madrid.

Unpublished

Piano solo: *Allegro de concert*.
Violin and piano: *Serenata andaluza*.
Violin, viola, violoncello and piano: *Piano quartet* (two movements – *Andante tranquillo* and *Ballabile*).
Flute, violin, viola, violoncello and piano: *Quintet* or *Fantasía*, based on Canto V of Mistral's poem *Mirèio* (two movements – 'Muerte de Elzear' and 'Danza fantástica').

The Allegro de concert was written for a Conservatoire competition for test pieces. Granados was the winner. The *Serenata andaluza* for violin and piano (evidently a different work from the similarly titled piano solo) was played at Cadiz in 1899 but has not survived. The mixed instrumental pieces were also played at Cadiz that year, the performers including Viniegra and Falla.

Falla's unpublished and unperformed *zarzuelas* were:
Limosna de amor; *El corneta de órdenes* (in collaboration with Amadeo Vives); *La cruz de Malta* (in collaboration with Amadeo Vives); and *La casa de Tócame Roque*.

They were probably written between 1900 and 1902. Only for *Tócame Roque* did Falla have any affection. He used a fragment in the Corregidor's Dance in *The Three-Cornered Hat*, and hoped unavailingly to find time to reconstruct the overture from memory. Roland-Manuel describes the overture as 'frankly delicious with great syncopated chords and a second idea related to the most Spanish inspirations of Domenico Scarlatti'. It is not clear whether the autograph still existed at that time (Roland-Manuel's monograph on Falla appeared in 1930) or whether Falla used to play it from memory.

The one really important and representative work of these early years was the opera *La vida breve*. Since it was not performed until 1913, and since Falla to some extent enlarged and revised the score in France, it can more fittingly be described in the next section.

Paris, 1907–14

A young Spanish composer full of talent and hope could not have chosen a more appropriate year than 1907 to arrive in Paris. Albéniz, who was living there, had reached the fourth book of his *Iberia* for piano. Debussy was engaged on his *Ibéria* (the third panel of the *Images* for orchestra). Ravel was writing *L'Heure espagnole* and the *Rapsodie espagnole*. Important new music not inspired by Spain included the opera *Ariane et Barbe-bleue* of Dukas. Fauré was about to start work on his opera, *Pénélope*. Debussy, with whom Falla had briefly corresponded from Madrid concerning a performance of the piano version of the *Danse sacrée et danse profane*, was away. The first eminent musician whom Falla met was Dukas – a fortunate choice. Debussy's paradoxes and sarcasms as an introduction to the musical world of Paris might have proved alarming to a stranger as shy, reserved and sensitive as Falla. Dukas was genial, wise and full of understanding. As his visiting card Falla had brought the score of *La vida breve*. Dukas was so impressed that he suggested the opera should be given at the Opéra-Comique – an event which did indeed come to pass, but only after a long wait.

Falla also met, for the first time, his compatriot Albéniz and another distinguished Spanish musician, the pianist Ricardo Viñes, champion of contemporary music and invaluable interpreter of Debussy and Ravel. For Ravel, though they held different views about religion, Falla felt admiration and warm affection. His intense admiration for Debussy's music shines through his own work. If, like others, he failed to come close to the elusive man, it may be significant that Debussy at that time was a controversial figure, living with but not yet married to Emma Bardac, and divorced from his first wife, who had tried to kill herself. Falla, though far from uncharitable, was conventional. The crisis in Debussy's life may explain why there seems to have been no particular contact between Fauré and Falla, Fauré (the 'musician of supreme serenity' as Falla described him) having been a warm admirer of Mme Bardac, for whom he had written the song-cycle *La Bonne Chanson*. At the period in question, relations between Fauré and Debussy were cool.

The leading musicians whom Falla did meet undoubtedly sensed the potential of the 'petit espagnol tout noir' as Dukas described him to Debussy. It is to the credit of both sides that by these impressive new friendships the little black Spaniard's musical personality was not crushed but affirmed. Of musical nourishment there was plenty, but the physical existence eked out by Falla with the aid of the inevitable lessons, accompanying, and translating work, was frugal. It was difficult to find cheap hotel rooms where piano practice was tolerated (Debussy complained that Falla changed his address almost as often as Beethoven). One of his biographers, Luis Campodonico, hints (without producing evidence) at some kind of breakdown in 1912 which, since Falla regarded it as punishment from above, led to still greater austerity. All the same, in the words of Federico Sopeña, editor of Falla's collected prose writings (published in English as *On Music and Musicians*), Paris 'made Manuel de Falla almost happy'.

The immediate fruits of Falla's stay were the four *Pièces espagnoles* for piano, begun before he left Madrid, published in 1909 by Durand on the recommendation of Dukas, Debussy and Ravel, thus permitting Falla to prolong his term in Paris, the *Trois Mélodies* on poems of Gautier, published the following year by Rouart, Lerolle, and *La vida breve*, recast in two acts. The contrast between the admiration of Dukas and others for the opera and the reluctance of opera managers to mount it would in itself almost explain a breakdown. A suitable translator was found in Paul Milliet, Treasurer of the Society of Authors. Albert Carré, director of the Opéra-Comique in Paris, showed interest but reached no decision (he could only stage a limited number of new works by non-French composers in any one season). Ricordi of Milan showed approval by offering Falla a contract, which he did not accept, for a new opera.[1] La Monnaie in Brussels signified interest but made no offer. Then, in 1912, Eschig of Paris accepted the score for publication and Falla accepted an offer from the Casino at Nice, whose management was preparing an extra grand season in rivalry with Monte Carlo, to stage the opera. The success of the Nice première in April 1913 stirred the Opéra-Comique into action. *La vida breve* was produced there (as *La vie brève*) in January 1914, with Carré's wife Marguerite as Salud.

News of this further success caused a sudden change of wind in Madrid. Doors hitherto closed were thrown open. The opera was given in November of the same year at the Teatro de la Zarzuela. After the first performance, Falla was accompanied home by torchlight. The outbreak of the First World War would in any case have forced him to leave Paris. He brought back to Madrid not only the revised opera but the as yet unperformed *Seven Spanish Folksongs* and sketches for what was to become *Nights in the Gardens of Spain*.

LA VIDA BREVE

Lyric drama in 2 acts, 4 scenes. Libretto by Carlos Fernández Shaw. French adaptation by Paul Milliet. First performed Nice, 1 April 1913, conductor J. Miranne. Published (as *La Vie brève*) by Max Eschig, Paris, 1913.

The opera is usually known by the Spanish title, meaning 'the short

[1] Mosco Carner in his biography of Puccini identifies this as *Anima allegra*, to an Italian libretto by Adami based on a play, *El genio alegre*, by the brothers Quintero.

life'. The action is set in Granada, at the turn of the century.

Act 1, Scene 1: The courtyard of a house in the gipsy district of El Albaicin. At one side a forge. Salud, who lives in the house with her grandmother, is impatiently awaiting her lover Paco. He has seduced her, promising marriage. The grandmother, full of mistrust, tries to calm her, warning her against loving too much. The scene now and later is punctuated by the voices of workers in the forge, striking their anvils and singing of the miserable lot of the poor folk who are born to be anvils rather than hammers. Salud takes up the thought in a short aria, 'Vivan los que rien!' (Happy those who laugh). Paco arrives, protesting his love. As the couple sing a duet, Tio Salvaor (Uncle Salvador, an old gipsy and the grandmother's brother) steals in. He has heard in the town that the very next day Paco is to marry a rich girl of his class. He and the grandmother go inside to discuss the situation. The lovers, Paco apparently as sincere as Salud, vow to meet again on the morrow.

Act 1, Scene 2: An interlude, played with the curtain up, depicting sunset and nightfall over Granada as seen from the Sacro Monte. There is no action but much writing for wordless off-stage chorus.

Act 2, Scene 1: A narrow street in the town. A patio is visible through the windows of one of the houses, belonging to the family of Carmela, Paco's bride. The wedding party is in progress. A *cantaor* with a guitar player in attendance sings *soleares* in honour of the couple. There is a dance (familiar in transcriptions as 'Spanish Dance No. 1'). Before it is over Salud appears, gazing into the courtyard. In a second aria, 'Alli está! Riyendo' (There he is – laughing), she sings of her grief at Paco's treachery and of her wish to die. The grandmother and Uncle Salvador join her. At the window, so that her voice can be heard inside, Salud repeats the workmen's hammer-and-anvil comparison from the first scene. She is determined to confront Paco.

Act 2, Scene 2: Inside the patio. The party continues with a second dance, this time choral (wordless again, except for cries of 'olé!', but this time on-stage). Carmela's brother Manuel, as head of the family, formally welcomes Paco. Carmela senses that something is wrong. Salvaor appears, leading Salud by the hand. To excuse his presence he offers to dance and sing for the company. Salud shrinks back, then suddenly finding courage, turns on Paco and denounces him. She advances towards him, ignoring his denials, and falls dead at his feet.

The music of *La vida breve* was conceived in haste, enthusiasm and high hopes at a time when Falla was overflowing with invention. The flow is not, as it would have been later, controlled by discrimination and a careful process of refinement. Nevertheless, the eclecticism and the youthful abundance are both endearing. They are buoyed up by a strong personality suddenly affirming itself. The libretto is weak. Fernández Shaw's experience in the field of *zarzuelas* did not help him much. Salud's tragedy moves to the arbitrary end in a series of spurts against a background of the sights and sounds of Granada drawn almost as elaborately as the Paris of Charpentier's *Louise*, which preceded Falla's opera by a few years. There are the expected lees of Wagner and of *verismo* with swerves into the idioms of Massenet, Puccini and the latter's Italian contemporaries. Other moments (not only the occasional chains of thirds on the flutes) suggest *Carmen*. The local colour, though not all of it helps, shows that Falla had quickly grown out of the salon style of the early pieces. The two dances, both in 3/4, placed dangerously close to one another, are skilfully differentiated. In the second dance (expanded in Paris on the advice of Messager), Falla does not try to cap the insidiously memorable tune pivoting on the dominant of the first dance, but relies on the extra colour added by the voices and on harmonic spice with a whiff of major–minor clashes.

Above all there is Salud, the only character drawn by the librettist in the round – Paco is a cipher, with little to do except sing one duet, the grandmother and Salvaor are background figures, the remainder even less important. In musical terms Falla sums up Salud in the opening bars of her first aria (Ex. 1). The general level of her music is so high that one forgives such lapses as the intrusion of Puccinian octaves later in the same aria. In less sensitive hands the character might have turned maudlin or termagant: even at her most distraught, Falla keeps Salud appealing and dignified. As for her sudden collapse, there is some if not enough motivation in her words about death in the second aria. The opera originally ended, it appears, with further curses flung at Paco by the grandmother and Salvaor. Debussy advised Falla to shorten these. He may have been right, but as it stands the end is abrupt.

Judging from a letter dated 16 August 1920 from the composer to G. Jean-Aubry, published in *The Chesterian* for October 1920, the revisions and extensions made in Paris did not amount to a great deal. Falla clears up possible misunderstandings due to an article

Ex.1 La vida breve, 'Vivan los que rien!'

by Turina in an earlier issue of the periodical. The change from one to two acts, Falla states, was made solely for the convenience of scene-changing. The interlude between the two scenes of the second act and the dance in the last scene were 'developed'. The rush to finish the opera for the Madrid competition had prevented his giving sufficient attention to the scoring of certain passages: these were now improved. But there was not 'the slightest fundamental modification' – in essence, what France heard was the opera that won the prize in Madrid.

La vida breve is scored for triple woodwind, 4 horns, 2 trumpets, 3 trombones, tuba, percussion, 2 harps, an on-stage guitar, strings.

PIÈCES ESPAGNOLES (FOUR SPANISH PIECES)
Piano solo. (1) Aragonesa, (2) Cubana, (3) Montañesa, (4) Andaluza. First

performed Paris, 27 March 1909, by Ricardo Viñes. Published by Durand, Paris, 1909.

The *Four Spanish Pieces* are the first example of Falla's mature style, of his concision, clear focus and instrumental writing at once resonant and lean. That this should be so is remarkable, because the set was nearly finished before he arrived in Paris, yet there is no apparent break in style. It is also noticeable because of the dedication of the *Pièces* to Albéniz, whom Falla first met in Paris where he was finishing his *Iberia*. Falla greatly liked and admired his older colleague, but though, at any rate in the *Pièces*, the basic musical language is similar, the use is different. Were it not for Falla's habitual courtesy one might almost think a mild corrective was being offered to the cornucopian *Iberia* – a lesson as it were in domestic economy. Albéniz proceeds by addition, throwing in more and more notes, having recourse to a third stave when his unreasonable demands on the ten fingers of the pianist's hands tend to clot the lines, sprinkling the pages with hairpins, and spattering them with pedal marks. Falla's indications are sparse and judicious. The contrapuntal lines, of which there are more than might be expected in music of an evocative and picturesque nature, are not designed to be half-hidden like the themes of Albéniz behind a surf of auxiliary notes, but to stand out clearly. Outlines are sharp.

'Aragonesa' summons attention with a burst of white-note chords, strongly accented. They lead to a lively tune in 3/8, a *jota* with a triplet on the second beat of the bar. The triplet persists throughout the piece. In the graceful coda (*un poco meno vivo*) the reiterated figure, slowly descending against rising staccato scales in the left hand, conveys a sense of gently swaying movement. 'Cubana' is a ravishing page in Latin American *guajira* rhythm, mixing 3/4 and 6/8. The rhythmic ambiguity persists, through a slightly faster middle section, lending suppleness to the way Falla slips in and out of the main key of A major. The music radiates a degree of relaxed happiness not often found in this composer. 'Montañesa' (subtitled 'Paysage') takes us to the north of the Peninsula with a sad, pastoral tune over a bell-like accompaniment 'quasi campani'. The middle section is a contrast, a perky Asturian folksong with groups of staccato semiquavers. The sad tune returns in rapt pianissimo. The final cadence, gently subsiding from E flat to D, is a beauty (Ex. 2).

'Andaluza' opens with a clanging fortissimo figure, with the grace

Ex.2 Pièces espagnoles, 'Montañesa'

Ex.3 Pièces espagnoles, 'Andaluza'

notes used by Falla in his piano writing from now on not so much for grace as for additional sonority. This is no longer the postcard Andalusia of the early *Serenata* but the harsher reality. After a stamping dance comes a sinuous *cante jondo* tune. The dance returns to be succeeded again by the song, dying away in the distance over a double ostinato in the left hand, one of Falla's loveliest inventions (Ex. 3). At the very end there is another ostinato in the bass, a two-note tick-tock figure descending from Mussorgsky through *Pelléas*.

Some writers have seen psychological significance in the fact that each of the *Four Spanish Pieces* ends quietly. Falla's temperament did not encourage him to rowdy, bangy endings like some by Albéniz, but there are several works by him that do not die away in silence, while of the twelve pieces in the *Iberia* of Albéniz, six in fact have quiet endings. It is more significant that Falla's soft closes do not become monotonous, that there is enough variety of mood in the *Pièces* to makes one forget the predominance of triple rhythms.

TROIS MÉLODIES

Voice and piano. Words by Théophile Gautier. (1) Les Colombes, (2) Chinoiserie, (3) Séguidille. First performance Paris, 1910, by Ada Adiny-Milliet and the composer. Published by Rouart, Lerolle, Paris, 1910.

The Gautier songs are one of Falla's neglected works. The reason may be that they are not Spanish but French in musical language as well as in text, French moreover in a fastidious way that wins the equally neglected and admirable songs of Roussel (and much of the later Fauré) more admiration than performance. They form a graceful and presumably intentional tribute to the styles of the composers from whom Falla learned so much in Paris. Gautier, author of *Le Voyage en Espagne*, was a natural and appropriate choice for a Spanish composer in love with France. The songs are precious in the fullest sense, as carefully worked as the enamels and cameos which Gautier used for the title (*Emaux et Camées*) of one of his collections of verse.

'Les Colombes' belongs to the world of Debussy and Ravel, with a hint of Fauré's prismatic harmony at 'elles quittent les branches Comme un collier' (Swarms of mad visions come winging down in the evening, to vanish with the first rays of light. My soul is like a green-plumed palm tree sheltering white doves through the night: in the morning they drop away like pearls from a necklace). 'Chinoiserie' belongs to an artificial, oriental vein worked by Debussy and Ravel, also by Roussel, whose first set of *Poèmes chinois* (Op. 10) dates from 1907–8. Debussy found the original opening of Falla's song too heavy. Falla suppressed the accompaniment, except for the opening chord and one later, until the voice reached the last word of the phrase 'Celle que j'aime à présent est en Chine' (The girl I'm in love with now is in China – she lives with her old parents in a porcelain tower on the Yellow River. She has slanting eyes, a narrow foot and long, red nails). 'Séguidille' is a lively essay in the French way of depicting Spain, somewhere between the rude enjoyment of Chabrier's *España* and the half-ironic local colour of Ravel's *L'Heure espagnole*. The subject is 'la véritable Manola', a cigarette-smoking, dancing beauty with tight skirt, large comb, a temperament of salt and pepper, and no thought for the morrow. Alza! Ola!

Madrid Again, 1914–20

The years of Falla's second stay in Madrid during and just after the First World War established him as a composer of international rank. Within weeks after the Madrid première of *La vida breve* in November 1914 Luisa Vela, the Salud of that production, gave the first performance of the *Seven Spanish Folksongs*. In a matter of weeks again, in April 1915, Madrid saw the first version of *El amor brujo*, at that stage a 'gitanería' or gipsy entertainment in two scenes for dancers (one of them also a singer) and instrumental ensemble. Pastora Imperio, a famous gipsy performer, had asked Falla and his friend Gregorio Martínez Sierra, playwright and theatre director, for 'a dance and a song'. They gave her more than that, but the mixture of a raw subject and a score distilled out of the essence of Andalusian folk music did not please the public (though, to Falla's contentment, Pastora's gipsy friends saw the point). Falla went to Barcelona, where the same production of *El amor brujo* was given, this time with success. He stayed with Martínez Sierra and his wife, and renewed acquaintance with the pianist, Frank Marshall. At Sitges on the coast, in congenial surroundings provided by another friend, the painter and writer Santiago Rusiñol, he finished *Nights in the Gardens of Spain*. From this time date the affection and regard

Falla felt for Barcelona, but not for Madrid. Later in 1915 he suffered a nervous depression or breakdown and spent some time in a clinic at Córdoba. There is a suggestion that the crisis was caused by a passion for Pastora Imperio, a rare example – if such was the case – of a breach in the armour of Falla's asceticism.

By March 1916, the scenario of *El amor brujo* had been recast in a single scene and the music adjusted and scored for a normal but still modest theatre orchestra. This version (the one now familiar) was given a concert performance in Madrid and soon became a favourite in the concert hall, but had to wait several years for a staging. The Russian impresario Serge Diaghilev, in Spain with the part of his ballet company that had not gone with Nijinsky to USA, asked Falla to collaborate with them, suggesting a danced version of the *Nights*. Falla preferred another subject, Alarcón's story *El sombrero de tres picos*, used by Hugo Wolf for his opera, *Der Corregidor*. Diaghilev agreed, allowing plans to proceed for independent presentation in Madrid of the first version, a mime-play by Martínez Sierra, with accompaniment by Falla for small ensemble, under the title *El corregidor y la molinera*. Diaghilev, while generally approving the result, suggested changes which in due course transformed the work into the ballet known in Spanish as *El sombrero de tres picos*, in French as *Le Tricorne*, in English as *The Three-Cornered Hat*.

Before the ballet was ready for performance, Falla embarked on the arrangement of music by Chopin for *Fuego fatuo*, a comic opera with spoken dialogue by María Martínez Sierra. The usual account of this mysterious venture is that Falla was tempted by the inducement of a reasonable chance of speedy production at a Madrid theatre, that he toiled through the summer, and then for some reason stopped short of completing the central act. María Martínez Sierra in her memoirs implies that it was Falla who wanted to orchestrate some Chopin (opportunities for doing this on a large scale come infrequently), and that she concocted a libretto at his request, writing the spoken dialogues and fitting the words of the sung numbers to the vocal lines Falla had extracted from Chopin. Of the allegations that the Madrid production fell through and that Falla offered the not quite complete work without success to other theatres in the capital and to Carré at the Opéra-Comique, she says nothing. She does, however, maintain that Falla became increasingly worried about the moral implications of the simple story, concerned with a young man torn between two loves, one good, one bad. Falla was as scrupulous in such matters as Beethoven. When he realised that the 'bad' woman's conduct was likely to involve the hero in adultery and when the librettist pointed out that a plot involving two 'good' women was unlikely to provide dramatic conflict of the kind needed for a comic opera, the scheme foundered. It is difficult to believe that Falla could have got as far as he did with the orchestration without realising the implications of the scenario.

There was more trouble over a proposal that he should write incidental music for *Don Juan de España*, a tragi-comedy by Gregorio and María Martínez Sierra. Falla procrastinated for so long (again there were moral scruples of a similar nature) that in desperation the couple asked their (and Falla's) friend Conrado del Campo to provide at least the minimum of music without which the play could not be performed. Falla, when he heard, was furious. There was an exchange of angry letters and a breach of friendship with the Martínez Sierras. Meanwhile *Fuego fatuo* was shut away until, many years after Falla's death, the score was examined and part of it turned into a concert suite. Because of work on the project, Falla declined an offer from Diaghilev to arrange a ballet on themes from Pergolesi. The commission for *Pulcinella* thus passed to Stravinsky.

The next year, 1919, was eventful. In July the Russian Ballet during their London season gave the first performance of *The Three-Cornered Hat*, splendidly mounted with choreography by the young Massine and scenery and costumes by another brilliant Andalusian, Picasso. Falla's stay in London was cut short by the news of his mother's serious illness. He hurried home to Madrid, but arrived too late. His father died later the same year.

The death of his parents meant there was no need to remain in Madrid. He had dreamed of settling in Granada, the Andalusian city he had drawn in such detail – before he had been there – in *La vida breve*. Though the definite move could not be made before the following year, Falla and his sister paid a long visit there in the latter half of 1919: among friends made during this stay were his future English biographer, J. B. Trend, and the young poet Federico García Lorca. Meanwhile Falla received two commissions. The first was a delicate gesture on the part of Arthur Rubinstein. Falla had been the intermediary (at the prompting, according to Pahissa, of Diaghilev's conductor, Ansermet) in a successful attempt to persuade the pianist to come to the aid of Stravinsky, in financial straits in Switzerland. Rubinstein, aware that Falla's own position was not rosy, sent cheques to both composers. Stravinsky responded with the *Piano-Rag-Music*, Falla with the *Fantasía baetica*, the last of his overtly Andalusian compositions. The other commission came from the Princesse Edmond de Polignac, who wanted an opera for her puppet-theatre in Paris. The outcome, *El retablo de maese Pedro*, was to mark the completion of a process already begun in *The Three-Cornered Hat*, an evolution from regional to national, from the particular to the general, and a growing interest in Spain's musical past. Between them the two assignments represent the end of one period and the start of another.

SIETE CANCIONES POPULARES ESPAÑOLAS
(SEVEN SPANISH FOLKSONGS)

Voice and piano. (1) El paño moruno, (2) Seguidilla murciana, (3) Asturiana, (4) Jota, (5) Nana, (6) Canción, (7) Polo. Words traditional. First performance Madrid, 14 January 1915, by Luisa Vela and the composer. Published by Max Eschig, Paris, 1922.

Pahissa tells that, about the time of the Paris production of *La vida breve*, Falla received two requests for advice. One was from a singer performing in the opera, who needed something Spanish for a projected recital, the other from a Greek singing-teacher who wanted to harmonise some Greek folksongs. Falla made one attempt himself, was agreeably surprised at the result, and decided to continue the experiment with songs from his own country. He used traditional tunes and words, with some retouchings. Either his knowledge (and memory) were already considerable or source material on Spanish folksong was more readily to hand in Paris than one might expect. The songs, ready by the time Falla left Paris for Madrid, are immaculately finished. Yet they must have needed research. In an article (the first of two) published in the Madrid periodical *Música* (I and II, 1953) the writer M. García Matos lists the sources in a footnote. They are too numerous to reproduce in full, but from the author's description it appears that the first and third songs are faithful copies of tunes and text, that in the second and sixth the tunes have been slightly retouched, the seventh retouched and expanded, the fifth considerably retouched, while the fourth is possibly a re-creation from various models. Further details are given in Livermore's *Short History of Spanish Music*. The set is dismissed in the *New Oxford History of Music* (vol. 10, *The Modern Age*) as 'a handful of folk-song arrangements', but these intensely imaginative re-creations are works of art on the level of Ravel's *Greek Folksongs* of 1907. In spite of the sophisticated finish, the ancient roots of Spanish popular life are almost tangible. This is not a cycle, but though the popularity of individual numbers is understandable, the seven are so well contrasted and balanced in mood and key that they only make their full effect in a complete performance. There exists an orchestration by Ernesto Halffter, and a more recent one (1978) by Luciano Berio, done with skill and sympathy for the orchestra Falla used for the revised *El amor brujo*, but without piano.

El paño moruno (The Moorish cloth). From Murcia – Falla later used the first four bars of the bass line (Ex. 4a) to characterise the (Murcian) miller in *The Three-Cornered Hat*. The entry of the voice is heralded by a typical *accacciatura* (Ex. 4b). (That fine cloth in the shop got stained. It will sell for less, for it has lost its value.)

Ex.4 Seven Spanish Folksongs, 'El paño moruno'

Seguidilla murciana. A popular dance-song in quick triple time. This one, as the name implies, comes from Murcia. Over fast running triplets the voice has mocking repeated notes, then graceful downward curves of a major or minor third. (Those who live in glass houses shouldn't throw stones. We're both muleteers, likely to meet on the road. Your inconstancy is like a coin passing from hand to hand, becoming so worn people think it is false and refuse it.)

Asturiana. A slow, sad lament from the Asturias in the north of Spain. The accompaniment hangs on the dominant of the home key, F minor. (To see if it would console me, I leant against a green pine. For seeing me weep – how green was that pine! – it wept too.)

Jota. One of the most widely known of Spanish dance-song forms, mainly associated with Aragon. The alternation of voice and instrument, the preludings of the latter in rapid 3/8 leading up to the entry of the voice in a slightly slower tempo, is characteristic. (Because we don't talk about it, they say we don't love one another, though they could consult your heart or mine. I must go now from your house and your window. Till tomorrow, whether your mother likes it or not.)

Nana. A lullaby of the oriental, Andalusian type. Descending figures in the piano part: a tonic pedal (the key is E major–minor, much inflected) sounded every time on the off-beat. (Sleep, boy; sleep, my love; sleep, little morning star of the morrow.)

Canción (Song). G major strikes freshly between the darker modes of the preceding and following songs. The 6/8 is unevenly stressed. (Those treacherous eyes of yours, I'm going to bury them. You think it costs 'nothing' to look at them. They say you don't love me, though that was not so before.)

Polo. Andalusian. Over strongly accented guitar figuration for the piano, the voice interjects savage, long-held cries of 'Ay!' and other expressions of despair, drawn out into *cante jondo* arabesques. (I bear in my heart a sorrow of which I shall tell no one. A curse on love and on those who made me feel it.)

NOCHES EN LOS JARDINES DE ESPAÑA
NIGHTS IN THE GARDENS OF SPAIN

Symphonic impressions for piano and orchestra. (1) En el Generalife (In the Generalife), (2) Danza lejana (Dance in the distance), (3) En los jardines de la Sierra de Córdoba (In the gardens of the Sierra de Córdoba). First performed Madrid, 9 April 1916, by the Orquesta Sinfónica de Madrid. Soloist, José Cubiles. Conductor, Enrique Fernández Arbós. Published by Max Eschig, Paris, 1922.

One of Falla's most immediately captivating works, concealing strange paradoxes and contradictions beneath a sensuous and exciting surface. Originally conceived in Paris for piano solo, Falla decided to recast the music for piano and orchestra. Extra-musical sources suggested for the *Noches* include a French poem by Francis Jammes and paintings by the Catalan artist Santiago Rusiñol, in whose house Falla worked on the score in the final stages (but unless Rusiñol's paintings were familiar to him before he went to Paris, the influence would have come too late to be more than an auxiliary source). The most convincing suggestion was passed to Ann Livermore by Falla's sister at a rehearsal of the *Nights* in Barcelona which Falla conducted, and which led Mrs Livermore to the opinion that 'the key to this score' was contained in three poems in the *Cantos de vida y esperanza* of the Nicaraguan writer, Rubén Darío (in the Colleción Austral edition the two 'Nocturnos', Nos. 5 and 32, and No. 6, 'Canción de otoño en primavera'). The poems are concerned with night-sounds heard in the distance and melancholy night-thoughts about the passing of youth and the difference between what was and what might have been. With Falla's ability to transform visual or literary stimulus into musical terms, they may have contributed to the headily subjective atmosphere of the *Nights*, which goes beyond objective illustration. There is an unmistakable feeling of Debussy, not of Debussy imitated but fully and deeply experienced. Paradoxically, the work that comes most readily to mind is the impersonal *La Mer*, but the mood of sensual ache is nearer the orchestral *Images* and nearest of all to the 'Parfums de la nuit' section of *Ibéria*, the last panel of the triptych. A further paradox – this Debussyan score is the one in which Falla came nearest to the formal ideals of the opposing faction in Paris, d'Indy and the Schola Cantorum (Falla had wanted to follow Turina's example and study there, but Dukas dissuaded him).

Though there are the traditional three movements, this is not a concerto but a work for piano and orchestra with an important, elaborate, yet discreet solo part combining the royal line of piano writing inherited by Debussy and Ravel from Chopin and Liszt with assimilated guitar effects and a hint or two of a recent, seminal score with an important piano part – *Petrushka*. Falla's first movement, named after the famous Generalife garden on the Alhambra hill at Granada, begins with a figure that sounds like an accompaniment but is a germinal theme. The first part is one of Falla's small interval inventions, with no step larger than a minor third:

Ex.5 Nights in the Gardens of Spain

The second part is more openly melodic:

Ex.6 Nights in the Gardens of Spain

This powerfully evocative movement is virtually a set of continuous variations on the theme. (In its new guise at letter 10 (min. score p. 17) Falla without realising it echoed a tune played day in day out by a blind beggar in the street outside the flats in Madrid where he and Vives lived – Vives found that he too had made involuntary use of the tune in a *zarzuela*.) Falla pointed out that the new theme at letter 7 of the second movement (min. score p. 42) derives from Ex. 6 and in turn becomes the first theme of the finale. Meanwhile much else in the work, including the minor-third call prominent in the second movement, can be related to Ex. 5 or Ex. 6.

Apart from the simmering opening and the last, ghostly appearance of the call, the 'Distant dance' does not sound particularly remote. It is joined by a short transition passage to the finale, which can be viewed either as a rondo or as Spanish *coplas* (couplets) with *estribillo* (refrain), the latter heard first and acting as the main rondo theme with the *coplas* as episodes. One of the episodes is a burst of *cante jondo* simulated by the piano playing in high octaves in a way Chopin used in his concerto finales – there is more Chopin in the *Nights* than appears at first, and not always in the obvious places. Another episode (letter 38, p. 32), based on the main rondo theme, hammers this, no doubt accidentally, into a shape resembling a passage in the finale of another cyclical work for piano and orchestra, d'Indy's *Symphonie cévenole* (min. score p. 60, bar 18).

Ex. 7
(a) Falla

(b) d'Indy

Authorities do not agree if what is happening in the Sierra de Córdoba represents a gipsy fiesta, though the physical vigour of the greater part of the movement suggests something of the kind. Towards the end the excitement quietens down: the *cante jondo* tune reappears over a throbbing bass pedal. The end, with the refrain blazing up briefly in augmentation before the music dies away, is filled with yearning.

The orchestra includes piano with 2 flutes, piccolo, 2 oboes, cor anglais, 2 clarinets, 2 bassoons, 4 horns, 2 trumpets, 3 trombones, tuba, timpani, harp, percussion (celesta, triangle, cymbals), strings. Falla uses the full orchestra with moderation but great effect. The naturally gifted orchestrator of *La vida breve* has become a master. Nothing is wasted, nocturnal sounds of some complexity are precisely noted, but there is no sound-painting for painting's sake. It may be an exaggeration to say that Falla's chamber-orchestra manner is already perceptible in the *Nights*, yet the quality of the writing can be fairly illustrated by a passage for five solo instruments (Ex. 8 overleaf).

The score was to have included an extra movement based on the Cadiz form of the Tango. This became the 7/8 'Pantomime' of *El amor brujo*. Perhaps as a result of the change of plan the balance of the three remaining movements is not entirely satisfactory, the moods of the second and third being a little too close to one another. Falla's sense of 'internal rhythm' may have alerted him to possible difficulties without providing an ideal solution. What he could not foresee was that the banal title, a child of the age of symphonic poems and picturesque orchestral writing, would wear less well than the music.

Ex.8

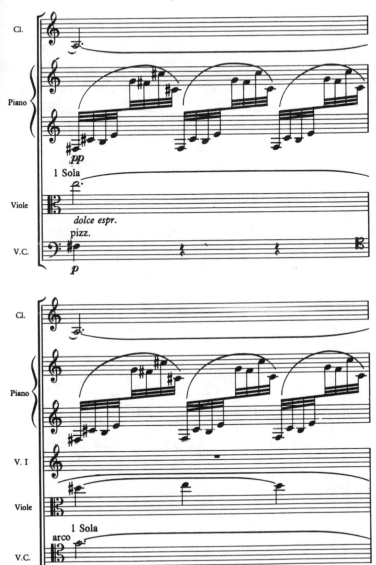

Ballet with songs in one act. Scenario by G. Martínez Sierra. First perform-
ance (see p. 25) Madrid, 15 April 1915, by Pastora Imperio and her company,
conductor Moreno Ballesteros. First (concert) performance of revised
version Madrid, 28 March 1916, by the Orquesta Filarmónica, conductor
Bartolomé Perez-Casas. First stage performance of revised version Paris
(Trianon-Lyrique), 22 May 1925, by Spectacles Bériza, with La Argentina,
Escudero and Georges Wague, conductor Falla. Published by J. &
W. Chester, London, 1921.

A young gipsy, Candelas, is haunted to the point of obsession by
the memory of her former lover, whose spirit persistently interrupts
the attempted love-making of her new admirer, Carmelo. Knowing
that the dead man was as unfaithful as he was jealous, Carmelo and
Candelas persuade another gipsy girl, Lucía, to use her charms to
distract the spirit's attention. Once the couple can seal their love
with a kiss, the spirit will be powerless.

The Introduction lunges into a fortissimo dotted-noted theme
associated with the spirit and his jealousy. 'En la cueva' (In the cave)
sets the scene, with a wailing theme for oboe that will appear again.
Canción del amor dolido (Song of love's sorrow) follows, a complaint
of unrequited love, with mournful cries of 'Ay!' (in the first version,
Pastora Imperio danced the role of Candelas and sang her songs;
in the revised version it is usual to have two performers, with the
singer at the side of the stage or in the orchestra pit). Three mysterious string chords, an agitated call on the muted trumpet, and some
glissandos announce the evil spirit and the *Danza de terror* (Dance of
terror). Here, as throughout the ballet, Falla uses his small forces,
especially the piano, in a masterly way to suggest the typical sounds
of Andalusian dancing – stamping, heel-tapping, clapping, and the
clack of castanets.

El círculo mágico (The magic circle). Candelas prepares to exorcise
the spirit by drawing a magic circle on the ground and by crossing
herself. This restrained, economical, tender page is the essence of
Falla. Midnight strikes (the bells are simulated: the real ones are
kept for the finale).

Danza ritual del fuego (Ritual fire dance). Smoky trills, wailing
oboes, baying horns, pounding chords on the piano. Much depends
in performance on exact observance of Falla's meticulous dynamic
markings. As the short Escena (scene) that follows shows, the ghost
is not yet laid.

Canción del fuego fatuo (Song of the will-o-the-wisp). Love as an *ignis fatuus*, enticing, never caught. The voice is strongly cross-rhythmed against the strings.

The *Pantomima* (Pantomime) opens with a forceful reiteration of the spirit's theme and calms down into a rocking 7/8 (*Andantino tranquillo*) with a tune on the solo cello; this is later taken up by first violins and violas, and is seductive enough to captivate the most determined evil spirit. This is the Cadiz tango movement originally intended for inclusion in *Nights in the Gardens of Spain*: note that the accompaniment is closely related to the opening theme of that work (Ex. 5), also to the *Círculo mágico* of the present one.

Ex.9 El amor brujo.
(a) 'Pantomime'

(b) 'The Magic Circle'

Lucía meanwhile is exercising her wiles. The faint reappearance on oboe and then muted trumpet of the spirit's theme implies that evil power is waning.

Danza del juego del amor (Dance of the game of love). A dance-song with cross-rhythms in the orchestral passages. The words are intended for the evil spirit – 'I am the voice of your destiny, the fire that consumes you, the sea in which you are shipwrecked.' The plot has worked. With the spirit's attention fully occupied by Lucía, Candelas and Carmelo can at last embrace in peace. Morning bells (real ones) peal out, and the voice joins in celebrating the happiness of the couple.

El amor brujo is now usually known by the Spanish title. The English translation *Love the Magician*, based on the French *L'Amour sorcier*, was unsatisfactory. The word *brujo* means sorcerer or wizard, but in this case there is presumably a double meaning, referring to the spirit of the dead lover but also to the power of love (more accurately, lust) that conquers. Pastora Imperio's mother, Rosario la Mejorana, fed Sierra and Falla with the tales and tunes of her race. They found Falla in a receptive mood, eager for Spain after years of absence in Paris. Of the original version, in two scenes with a slightly different scenario and scored for piano, flute, oboe, trumpet, horn, viola, cello and double bass one cannot speak until it sees the light again. But in the known version (flute, piccolo, oboe, 2 clarinets, bassoon, 2 horns, 2 trumpets, timpani, bells, piano and strings) Falla caught the feel of midnight witchcraft and gipsy hot-bloodedness with music of high colour and racing pulse that appeals to the general public while musicians admire the terse, swift, pungent, economical writing. The score bears no indication of location. Trend described how, some years after writing the work, Falla found in Granada an ideal setting for the ballet 'in a large white cave on the Sacro Monte, clean as a new pin under its perpetually renewed coats of whitewash and hung with a quantity of shining copper pans'. Yet according to information received from the family, neither version of *El amor brujo* was originally intended to be set at Granada but on 'the sea-coast somewhere in the Bay of Cadiz'. This would explain the subtitle 'The Fisherman's story' of the 'Magic circle' number, the decision to use the Cadiz tango music for this ballet and not for the *Nights*, also for the fact so far not alluded to that the fortissimo appearances of the spirit theme sound uncommonly like crashing waves. There is nothing necessarily inconsistent in Falla's remark to Trend. Possibly the maritime setting, having served as initial stimulus, had ceased to interest him.

EL SOMBRERO DE TRES PICOS
(THE THREE-CORNERED HAT)

Ballet in two scenes. Scenario by G. Martínez Sierra, after the story by Alarcón. First performance, as *El corregidor y la molinera* (mime-play in two tableaux), Madrid, 7 April 1917, conductor Joaquín Turina. First performance of revised version (as *The Three-Cornered Hat*) London, Alhambra Theatre, 22 July 1919, by the Ballets Russes, conductor Ernest Ansermet. Published by J. & W. Chester, London, 1921.

The Introduction was added in London, to give the audience time to admire Picasso's drop-curtain. In the orchestra, drums and trumpets. On stage, handclaps, castanets, cries of 'Olé!' and a distant voice warning of trouble. The curtain rises on a terrace outside a mill on the outskirts of a small Andalusian town. The miller and his wife go happily about their business. She is young and a beauty, he is ugly. Each has a typical theme. The Miller's (he comes from Murcia) is borrowed from the first of the *Seven Spanish Folksongs*. His Wife's – she is from Navarre – is a tempting snatch in *jota* rhythm.

Ex.10 The Three-Cornered Hat

They are deeply in love, but neither can resist testing that love by flirting. A dandy passes by, ogling the wife. There follows a procession bringing the local magistrate or Corregidor, wearing his three-cornered hat as badge of office. His theme is a pompous bassoon solo. In his train are his wife in a sedan-chair, and some *alguacils* or policemen. The miller's wife attracts the Corregidor's eye, but when he slips back alone she pretends not to notice him, being occupied with dancing a *fandango*. Eventually she greets him, mock-ceremoniously, in an old-fashioned minuet – the period is the early nineteenth century, the time of Goya. She teases him with a bunch of grapes, held just out of reach. The Corregidor chases her, trips up, is helped to his feet, then departs in an ill-humour. The miller and his wife resume the *fandango* under the watching eye of an *alguacil*. In the second scene the neighbours foregather (it is St John's Eve) to drink wine and dance *seguidillas*. The Miller dances a *farruca*, a late-comer to the score, written to provide Massine with a solo, an exhibition of tough masculinity for the benefit no doubt of the wife – and of the absent Corregidor. However the police appear, knocking on the gate like Beethoven's Fate, to arrest the miller and take him away. The distant, warning voice is heard again, this time adding cuckoo-calls. The Corregidor steals in, limping but pertinacious. He stumbles and falls into the millstream, emerging drenched but still determined. The miller's wife, indignant then amused, threatens him with a gun then runs off, suddenly frightened. The Corregidor lays out his clothes to dry before taking shelter in the miller's house. The miller, who has escaped his captors, returns alone, sees the clothes (and the hat), fears the worst and decides to revenge himself by wearing the clothes and going to serenade the Corregidor's wife. So the Corregidor, when he creeps shivering out of the house, is forced to put on the miller's clothes. During the whirl of activity that follows he is arrested in error by his own men. For this final dance the neighbours reassemble. Once identities are sorted out, the miller and his wife are reconciled. The *jota* theme is at last allowed to blossom fully. The dandy returns with a straw effigy of the Corregidor, which is joyfully tossed in a blanket. (Goya painted a similar episode.) The physical élan of this finale almost obscures the skill with which Falla interweaves the main themes of the score – even the cuckoo-calls recur. (A more detailed description of the scenario will be found in the miniature score.)

The orchestra is larger than that for *El amor brujo*. Falla uses 2 flutes, piccolo, 2 oboes, cor anglais, 2 clarinets, 2 bassoons, 4 horns, 3 trumpets, 3 trombones, tuba, harp, celesta, piano, xylophone, timpani, percussion, strings, and a mezzo-soprano off-stage. Even so, Falla keeps the third and fourth horns and the trombones in reserve for the finale. The texture is richer, more luminous, than in the previous ballet. There is another difference. In *El amor brujo* Falla caught the essence of a certain kind of Andalusian folk music without using a single traditional tune. *El sombrero*, on the other hand, is stuffed with themes and phrases of popular origin, not reproduced whole or almost whole as in the *Seven Spanish Folksongs* but absorbed into the fabric. García Matos in the article mentioned on p. 28 lists many sources; there is more information in Pahissa and Demarquez. Some of the fragments come from popular tunes of presumably no great antiquity, others from children's street songs. Not all are Andalusian. The leading themes from Murcia and Navarre have been referred to. One is Andalusian that doesn't sound so, the diatonic bassoon phrases associated with the Corregidor, first heard at letter 29, p. 62 min. score.

Ex.11

42

The deliberately stiff, old-fashioned dance performed by that worthy before he tumbles into the water in the second scene was taken from Falla's unpublished and unperformed *zarzuela*, *La casa de Tócame Roque*. A subsidiary theme in the Neighbours' Dance (letter 5, p. 105 min. score) was noted down by Falla from a blind musician at Granada during a journey round Spain which he made in the summer of 1917 in the company of Diaghilev, the choreographer-elect Massine and a flamenco dancer, Felix Fernández García, whom Massine had befriended on an earlier visit to Granada. Diaghilev had taken Felix into the Ballets Russes so that he could teach Andalusian steps and style to Massine and the company (see Richard Buckle, *Diaghilev*, London 1979). The journey, which covered parts of the north and centre of the peninsula as well as the south, brought new experiences to Falla as well as the two Russians: it may have been a factor in Falla's gradual shift from regional to national (in which *El sombrero* marks an important stage). *El sombrero* is a mosaic, but the result is so spontaneous that the various origins of the music do not draw attention to themselves. To give some indication of the way the mosaic was fitted together, one may quote the first phrase of the tune that opens the Neighbours' Dance in Scene Two and the source García Matos adduces for it, a gipsy song from Granada, sung at weddings after ritual confirmation of the bride's virginity – note that the flattened seventh is already present (Ex. 12a and b).

Ex.12
(a) 'The Neighbour's Dance'

43

Of the two orchestral suites drawn from the ballet and often heard in the concert hall, the first, 'Scenes and Dances', consisting of (1) Introduction – afternoon, (2) Dance of the Miller's Wife (Fandango), (3) The Corregidor, (4) The Grapes, includes most of Scene One. The second, 'Three Dances', includes the three big numbers in Scene Two: (1) The Neighbours, (2) The Miller's Dance (Farruca), (3) Final Dance; it omits several pages of inventive and finely-worked music placed in the full score between the Miller's Dance and the Finale, giving an incomplete idea of the ballet as a whole. Unfortunately, it is the more frequently played of the two suites.

The differences between the two ballets are not confined to the methods of composition. *El amor brujo* is concerned with the supernatural, with private happenings, indoors (at least in a cave), at night, with no one present except the intimates of those concerned. *The Three-Cornered Hat* is about the natural behaviour of ordinary people, set in the open air, in a place overlooked by passers-by. The atmosphere is not secretive but sunny – the Neighbours' Dance being filled with the contentment of relaxation after work at an hour when in Mediterranean countries walls and baked earth give off the heat absorbed during the day. The differences extend to the respective fates of the ballets. *El amor brujo*, in the revised version, a success in the concert hall from the start, has been choreographed by almost every Spanish dancer of note from La Argentina to Antonio, and by many distinguished non-Spaniards as well. Yet though La Argentina's version (Paris, 1925) was famous in its time, it has not outlasted its creator, and no other version has won anything like the celebrity of the collaboration of Massine and Picasso which made *The Three-Cornered Hat* one of the corner-stones of the Diaghilev Ballet's repertory and one of the outstanding examples of his ideal of a fusion of dancing, music and décor. There may be a musical reason. The polish, concision and suggestive power of the score of *El amor brujo* seems to contradict the improvisatory nature of flamenco dancing. Physical movement is so precisely suggested that the real thing has little to add – a similar difficulty (from a choreographer's point of view) exists with Ravel's music in dance forms. Lastly, each ballet benefits from the presence of one number from the world of the other. In *El amor brujo* it is the 'Pantomime', honey injected into vinegar; in *The Three-Cornered Hat* it is the assertive Miller's *farruca*, like home truths suddenly spoken in a world of play and pretence.

Piano solo. First performance New York, 1920, by Arthur Rubinstein. Published by J. & W. Chester, London, 1922.

The work Falla wrote in 1919 for Rubinstein was his last for solo piano with the exception of the *Homage to Dukas* and the unfamiliar *Canto de los remeros de la Volga*. With the partial exception of the *Homage to Debussy* for guitar, it is the last work of his Andalusian period – written a year before he settled in the province, at Granada. And with the exception of the *Allegro de concert* (unpublished) of 1902, the Fantasy is Falla's sole contribution to the virtuoso piano tradition in which he was trained. There is virtuoso writing in the piano part of the *Nights*, but the effect is deliberately restrained. No one without thorough knowledge of the instrument's capabilities could have written the piano part in *El amor brujo*, but the virtuosity there lies in the power of suggestion obtained by the simplest means. The *Fantasía baetica* (Baetica was the Roman name for the province; the adjective is also spelt *bética*) is a bravura piece in the line of Balakirev's *Islamey* and Debussy's *L'Isle joyeuse*.

The Fantasy is in ABA form with B a short Intermezzo. Guitar figurations transformed into pianistic terms abound, but the piece does not depend on them alone. Other passages evoke the harpsichord, Scarlatti as it were, rewritten by Bartók (Ex. 13).

Ex.13 Fantasía Baetica

That the piano can suggest a guitar (since Debussy showed the way in his instinctive evocations of Andalusia) or a harpsichord is not surprising. What is uncanny is Falla's ability to make the keyboard suggest the long-drawn, husky, minutely inflected lines of *cante jondo* singers, doing so moreover less by sustained legato than by percussive writing with the addition of incisive grace-notes:

Ex.14 Fantasía Baetica

Lento di nuovo

In the outer parts of the Fantasy the style is aggressive and dissonant, the mood savagely exultant, the modal colouring Phrygian. The Intermezzo has a strange, withdrawn quality with a melody that begins like one of Falla's small-interval themes then slowly uncoils itself over the span of a ninth with an effect of brooding stillness broken by the abrupt return of the original material. There is a substantial recapitulation, with coda. This repetition emphasises a certain static, insistent, tail-biting quality in the music shared with the kind of Andalusian dancing it often conjures up. The dance critic André Levinson, analysing in his essay on La Argentina the difference between the turned-out movements of Western classical dance and the opposing characteristics of the Andalusian kind, summed up the latter in the following terms: 'curved lines, ellipses and spirals . . . the movements *concentric*; the knees for preference close together and bent, the arms curving inward enveloping the torso, everything concentrated, converging.' The *Fantasía* has recently become popular after years of neglect. An orchestral version by Ernesto Halffter exists but has not been published.

FUEGO FATUO (FIREFLY)

Suite for orchestra, arranged by Antoni Ros Marbá from the unperformed and unpublished comic opera in three acts by María Martínez Sierra, music by Falla after Chopin. First performance of the suite, Granada Festival, 1 July 1976, by the National Orchestra of Spain, conductor Antoni Ros Marbá. Unpublished.

The existence of *Fuego fatuo* was known: Falla never erased the work from his list of works. It has generally been described as 'based on themes of Chopin', but when the score turned up in the Falla archives and was duly examined by Enrique Franco and other expert musicians it transpired that what Falla had done was to orchestrate complete piano works (with some abridgements) and to provide one piece listed as 'original, in the style of Chopin'. Falla respected Chopin's melodic lines, leaving, it seems, María Martínez Sierra, who was responsible for the libretto, to fit in the words. The genesis of the work sounds unpromising, yet the examiners were so impressed with what they found that it was decided to make an orchestral suite out of Acts One and Three, the scoring of Act Two being incomplete. Only slight adjustments, such as the addition of the vocal line when not already doubled by the orchestra, proved necessary. The works of Chopin selected by Falla for the outer acts and used in the suite are as follows:

(1) Waltz in A flat Op. 64 No. 3, with a theme from the Scherzo in B flat minor, Op. 31
(2) Scherzo in E, Op. 54 (central section only)
(3) Mazurka in C, Op. 24 No. 2
(4) Bolero, Op. 19
(5) Mazurka in B minor, Op. 33 No. 4, leading without break to
(6) Tarantella, Op. 43
(7) Mazurka ('Życzenie', No. 1 of the Polish Songs, Op. 74)
(8) Berceuse, Op. 57 (considerably shortened)
(9) Ballade in F minor, Op. 52
(10) Barcarolle, Op. 60

Some of the above are transposed, and there are a few minor alterations apart from those listed. No. 7 is taken direct from the first of the Polish Songs and not, as had previously been stated, from Liszt's piano transcription. The orchestration, for 2 flutes, oboe, cor anglais, 2 clarinets, 2 bassoons, 2 horns, 2 trumpets, 3 trombones, percussion, piano (4 hands), harp and strings, is of masterly sobriety. There is telling but brief use in the Tarantella of the piano duet. Otherwise, in an age of colourful orchestral arrangements such as the Rossini–Respighi *La Boutique fantasque*, ear-tickling effects are avoided. The superimposition of a theme from the B flat minor Scherzo on the middle section of Waltz in No. 1 is not as crude as it sounds. Falla's understanding of Chopin goes deep. Gerald Abraham once wrote: 'It was actually only the generation after Wagner – the generation of Szymanowski and Skryabin – which really discovered how to write Chopinesque music for the orchestra.' To those names, different as his palette is from theirs, must be added Falla's. The unfinished second act reputedly used (1) a Berceuse, 'original, in the style of Chopin', (2) Etude in E, Op. 10 No. 3, (3) Mazurka in A flat, Op. 7 No. 4, (4) Ballade in G minor, Op. 23, (5) Waltz in A flat, Op. 42 and Mazurka in A minor, Op. posth. (ded. Gaillard), (6) Etude in C minor, Op. 10 No. 12.

MISCELLANEOUS WORKS

A small work of the period that for a long time remained unpublished (perhaps because there is no obvious Spanish colour) is the song 'Oración de las madres que tienen a sus hijos en brazos' (Prayer for mothers who carry their sons in their arms), words by G. Martínez Sierra, first performed Madrid, 8 February 1915, by Josefina Revillo and the composer. The words are a prayer to the Infant Jesus on behalf of mothers who do not want their infant sons to become soldiers when they grow up. The voice part moves smoothly over a subdued accompaniment. Debussy's 'Noël des enfants qui n'ont plus de maison' (Carol for homeless children) on a similar subject was written a year later. There is no apparent connection. There is however some musical similarity between Falla's song and the second of Debussy's *Trois Ballades de François Villon* of 1910.

The years of friendship with Gregorio and María Martínez Sierra produced one other song, a tiny 'Canción Andaluza' called 'El pan de Ronda' (Ronda bread), the result of an excursion to Ronda with the Martínez Sierras and the purchase there of some crusty bread from a street-stall, which inspired María to improvise some couplets, subsequently set to music by Falla for voice and piano. The idiom is unmistakably Andalusian, with an unexpected upward twist for the voice at the end. The song was to have been part of a cycle that remained unwritten. Falla also wrote incidental music for a translation of Shakespeare's *Othello* produced under the direction of Martínez Sierra at Barcelona in 1915, and more music for two plays by him, *Amenecer* (1914) and *La pasión* (1916). None of this has survived except a *soleá* for the last-named play.[1]

Granada, 1920–39

With his faithful sister María del Carmen, who was to remain with him as housekeeper and amanuensis for the rest of his life, Falla moved to Granada in 1920 to make his home there. After staying in pensions on the Alhambra hill, they found an enchanting small house on the southern slopes near the Alhambra Palace Hotel, in a secluded street named Antequera alta. The house, now a museum of personal mementoes, is small and simple, with a small patio and a garden so cunningly laid out on various levels that it seems larger than it really is. House and garden have a spectacular view of the Sierra Nevada mountains and the plain called La Vega. Above the miniature garden there is now a larger one, leading to a modern building, the Centro 'Manuel de Falla' (see page 7).

Falla was no longer writing Andalusian music and had become an international figure, but he had not come to Granada to rest on his laurels. A concern for the social usefulness of music encouraged him to take part in local activities. His literary friends there included Lorca, already in spite of his youth a passionate theatrical animator: Falla helped him with music for the plays he put on and for puppet shows staged in his private theatre – excellent preparation for *El retablo*. Lorca was a good musician, a competent pianist and a better arranger of folk songs than many of Falla's epigones. Unfortunately their collaborations were not intended to be durable (though Manuel Orozco found an unpublished text of a two-act puppet opera by Lorca, *La comedianta*, with marginal annotations by

[1] Both Martínez Sierra songs are published by Union Musical Española (Madrid, 1980) in Vol. 1 of *Obras desconocidas*.

Falla for the music),[1] and since they were neighbours and could meet frequently when they were both in Granada, little correspondence between them has survived. Falla and Lorca were two of the moving spirits in the *cante jondo* competition held at Granada in 1922. There was reason, then as now, to fear that the old, uncorrupted traditions of Andalusian song were endangered by vulgarisation and commercialisation. The municipality voted funds, the Centro Artístico undertook the organisation, Lorca gave a public lecture, Falla lent his name to a prefatory pamphlet. Professionals were excluded from participation (but not from attendance) unless they were under twenty-one – which enabled them, however, to enter their best pupils. One of the most acclaimed of the winners was Antonio Bermúdez, a seventy-year-old countryman who had walked for three days to attend. Falla greatly admired his style and carefully preserved recordings made by Bermúdez during his visit: since he had given up singing for many years owing to a lung complaint, he had not learned decadent ways and, in Falla's opinion, was 'an arsenal of true song'.[2]

Another attempt to stir up musical life in the Peninsula was Falla's initiative in the creation (with the aid of Eduardo Torres, the choirmaster of Seville cathedral, and of the Sevillan cellist Segismundo Romero) of a chamber orchestra to play the classics and modern scores not only in Seville but in other towns where there was little or no opportunity of hearing such music. These players, with the assent of the Princesse de Polignac, were allowed to give the first (concert) performance of the newly completed *El retablo de Maese Pedro*, which they were later to tour round Spain in the puppet version. By then they had been christened 'Orquesta Bética de Cámara' and the regular conductorship had been offered to a promising young composer, Ernesto Halffter. The nucleus of the orchestra was about the size – double woodwind etc. – for which Falla liked to write. For them, or so his letters to Romero imply, he prepared a version of the overture which Rossini attached to *Il barbiere di Siviglia*, dispensing with the trombones (a later accretion).

[1] Lorca's (incomplete) text, now published (Madrid, 1981) as *Lola la comedianta*, is a one-act comic opera libretto for human performers, not puppets. One of the manuscript drafts (reproduced in this critical edition by Piero Menarini) contains verbal annotations and two tiny musical fragments in Falla's hand.

[2] See Eduardo Molina Fajardo, *Manuel de Falla y el 'cante jondo'* (Granada, 1962, reissued 1976).

The first years at Granada, which saw the writing of the *Homage to Debussy*, the *Puppet Show*, *Psyché*, the Harpsichord Concerto and the *Soneto a Córdoba*, were busy as well as productive. In his enchanting setting, Falla received visitors from near and far. One who had a stimulating effect was the harpsichordist Wanda Landowska. Her playing of early Spanish music to Falla and friends, on one occasion on the Alhambra, further increased an interest in old instruments which had already been awakened by Falla's examination of some specimens in a private collection at Toledo – in these days when the harpsichord has become ubiquitous again, it is difficult to imagine the novelty of Landowska's pioneering work for the instrument. Falla rewarded her with a harpsichord part in the *Puppet Show*, followed by the solo part of the Concerto.

Granada provided congenial friends among his own and the younger generation. He needed quiet and solitude for his work. Yet in his letters to J. B. Trend (later Professor of Spanish at Cambridge), unpublished but preserved in Granada University Library, with their reiterated greetings to Edward Dent and enquiries after Vaughan Williams – whose music, or such of it as he knew, evidently appealed to Falla – there is a note of loneliness, of hunger for cosmopolitan company. This, apart from the necessity of earning money by playing and conducting, may be one reason why, when his health was already beginning to decline, Falla travelled so much inside and outside Spain. He went, more than once, to London, to Paris (notably in 1923 for the first staged performance of the *Puppet Show* at the house of the Princesse de Polignac), Italy and Switzerland for ISCM· or other contemporary music festivals or premières of his works. On one of these journeys, in 1926, the project of *Atlántida* was conceived: 1926 and 1927 (before he began work on the score and his output accordingly diminished) form a watershed during the Granada period.

There were still visits abroad. Links with France remained close. Falla was made Chevalier of the Legion of Honour in 1928. Six years later,.on the recommendation of Dukas, he succeeded Elgar as a member of the Institut de France. Other developments were less encouraging. As his health grew worse (the main trouble appears to have been tubercular), the political situation in Spain declined. So did the amenities of Granada: the paradise turned out to have serpents, and they made a noise. Shortly before the visits to Mallorca he was, in his own words, 'disabled' for two months by a neighbouring gramophone. When there were fairs at the bottom of the hill, he could hear the roundabouts. More than once Falla had assured the Mallorcan priest, writer and musician Juan María Thomas that he would visit the island. Eventually he made the decision and, with María del Carmen in attendance, stayed in the village of Génova above Palma in 1933 and 1934. Thomas directed a local choir of some standing. For them Falla wrote the *Balada de Mallorca* and made a transcription of an *Ave Maria* of Victoria and of part of Vecchi's *Amfiparnaso*. On his return home he stopped in Barcelona to conduct a concert of his music.[1] This was his last public appearance in Spain. The outbreak of the Civil War in July 1936 found him ill at Granada.

This ultra-conservative man had friends on both sides. Luis Campodonico describes Falla's view of the Civil War as 'short and simplistic. For him, Spain was the Spain of the Catholics.' But not, if he could help it, of warlike Catholics. As a much-respected national figure he was courted by Right and Left. When some of the local militia of Granada begged him to write them a 'martial hymn' all that this least martial of men was willing to give them was an arrangement for unison voices of the 'Song of the Almogávares' in Pedrell's *Los Pirineos*. Though the march is said to have been tried out at the Staff College at Burgos, it was not adopted. The government, which had appointed Picasso Keeper of the Prado in Madrid, offered Falla the Presidency of the Institute of Spain, which he declined. The shooting of Lorca in 1936 was a grievous blow. Falla did not know that the poet had returned to Granada from Madrid, and when he heard rumours of his arrest he attempted, in spite of his precarious health, to intervene with the authorities; but it was too late. A period of severe nervous prostration was the result.

During the years at Granada, Falla's already strong religious convictions increased in intensity. Various writers commented on his emaciated, spiritualised appearance. One compared him to 'a monk by Ribera retouched by Zurbarán', another to a reincarnation

[1] So say Sagardía, Demarquez and Orozco, but no trace of this concert has so far materialised. On his way to Majorca, however, for his second visit, on 2 December 1933, Falla conducted a performance at the Liceo in Barcelona of the *Noches* (with Marshall as soloist) after *La vida breve* and *El amor brujo* (both conducted by Lamote de Grignon), which were in the repertory that season.

of St John of the Cross, 'alike even in their bodily lightness and in their outbursts . . . Falla was a saint and doctor of music just as Fray Juan was saint and doctor of the Church' – more than three centuries earlier San Juan de la Cruz had been prior of the former Carmelite Convent of the Martyrs on the hill above Falla's house. Falla lived simply, humbly, charitably. When asked why he gave alms to an old woman in the neighbourhood suspected of communist connections, he replied simply 'because I am a Christian'. Without intruding them on others, he took his religious duties seriously. Poulenc, among others, noted how in church he would plunge into prayer with the total absorption of a mystic. He came to regard his stage works as sinful, and feared their bad influence on others. In 1932 he made a will which insisted that these works should be performed in accordance with the strictest Christian principles, and that they should only be accompanied by other works of suitably high moral tone (later that year he was distressed to find the *Puppet Show* was sharing a programme at the Venice Festival with the *Maria Egiziaca* of Respighi – his scruples were moral, not musical). In 1935 he added a codicil to the will which, had it not proved inoperable owing to the existing contracts with his publishers, would have deprived the public of the chance to see staged performances of his operas or ballets, or for that matter of *Atlántida*.

The Civil War ended in April 1939. Not unnaturally the period had been unproductive. Some work was done on *Atlántida*, and after a slight improvement in his condition in 1938, he finished the suite *Homenajes*. Shortly after the end of the war Falla was invited by the Spanish Cultural Institute of Buenos Aires to conduct four concerts of Spanish music in honour of the twenty-fifth anniversary of the Institute's foundation. After consultation with his doctors, he accepted. With his sister he sailed from Barcelona on 2 October, seen off by Romero, Marshall and other close friends. With him he carried the torso of his *Atlántida*. Appropriately the sea-route took them through the Straits of Gibraltar and across the legendary site of drowned Atlantis. The concerts in Buenos Aires covered the sixteenth century as well as contemporary music. The fourth programme, devoted entirely to Falla, included the first performance of *Homenajes*. Buenos Aires was welcoming but big and noisy. The concerts were successful but their preparation and execution, in spite of invaluable collaboration from the Argentinian composer and conductor Juan José Castro, was exhausting for a man as frail as Falla. He was advised to go to the hills. Eventually, not before he had made a brief return visit to Buenos Aires to conduct two radio concerts, he and María del Carmen settled in a small villa at Alta Gracia in the Argentinian province of Córdoba, in a landscape that reminded him of his beloved Andalusia. Here, in isolation and increasing infirmity, he was to spend his few remaining years.

EL RETABLO DE MAESE PEDRO
(MASTER PETER'S PUPPET SHOW)

Musical and scenic version of an episode from *El Ingenioso Cavallero Don Quixote de la Mancha* by Miguel de Cervantes. Words adapted from Cervantes by the composer. First (concert) performance Seville, 23 March 1923, for the Sociedad Sevillana de Conciertos, conductor Falla. First (private) puppet performance Paris (in the house of the Princesse de Polignac), 25 June 1923, by the Golschmann Orchestra, conductor Wladimir Golschmann. First public puppet performance Clifton (Bristol), 14 October 1924, Sargent conducting. Published by J. & W. Chester, London, 1924.

The scene is the stable of an inn, with a trestle theatre belonging to a travelling showman, Master Peter. In the theatre small puppets perform a drama about the Christian Princess Melisendra, daughter of the Emperor Charlemagne, rescued from Moorish captivity by her husband Gayferos, a knight at the Emperor's court. Master Peter and his Boy, Quixote and his squire Sancho Panza and other onlookers are represented by larger puppets, for which singers or mimes wearing masks may be substituted. There are three singing roles: Master Peter (tenor), the Boy (treble or soprano) and Quixote (*basso cantante* or baritone). If the large puppets are used, the singers are placed in the orchestra. (The action is continuous. Scenes are named and numbered here for the convenience of the reader.) After a skirl from piercing oboes over percussion at rhythmic odds with them, Master Peter announces the play. While his audience take their seats we hear a rustic *sinfonia* like a much-expanded version of the introduction to *The Three-Cornered Hat*. Horns, trumpets, drums and the plucked instruments (harpsichord and the paler harp-lute) are prominent. Master Peter begs silence as the Boy starts to describe:

Scene 1. The Court of Charlemagne. Instead of going to the rescue of Melisendra, Gayferos is playing chess. His father-in-law the

Emperor rebukes him and prods him into action. Gayferos calls for his armour and tries to borrow a sword from his companion-at-arms, Roldán. The latter refuses but offers to go with Gayferos, who haughtily declines and prepares to leave alone. (The Emperor's solemn *gallarda* is based on one of the *cantigas* of Alfonso the Wise.)

Scene 2. Melisendra. From her prison in a tower at Saragossa the captive scans the horizon. An amorous Moor steals a kiss but is seen by the Moorish king, Marsilius, who orders him to be punished. Melisendra's melancholy theme, alternating 3/4 and 6/8, passing from instrument to instrument, is an 'old romance' taken from Salinas and quoted in the first volume of Pedrell's *Cancionero*, typically Fallesque in its plaintive quality and small compass.

Ex.15 Master Peter's Puppet Show

When the Boy, informing the audience that the punishment of three hundred stripes is to be administered forthwith in the public square, adds an uncomplimentary remark about Moorish justice, Don Quixote tells him to mind his own business and get on with the story. 'Too much counterpoint ruins the lute-strings', adds Master Peter.

Scene 3. The Moor's Punishment. The flogging takes place to an oriental-sounding march based on an old children's song. Over a background of softly clashing percussion, harpsichord and harp-lute, penetrating woodwind timbres add an acrid polytonal colouring that will be heard again, in more extreme form, in the Concerto.

Scene 4. The Pyrenees. The Boy announces the departure, on horseback, of Gayferos. The orchestra sets the scene with a galloping rhythm in fast triplets (compare the 'Seguidilla' of the *Seven Spanish Folksongs*) and horn and trumpet calls resounding through the hills – an admirable example of Falla's ability to draw a large sound from a few instruments. When the Boy resumes, he tells how Melisendra spies Gayferos from afar. Not recognising him she asks for news of her husband, whereupon the knight reveals himself and she leaps into his arms.

Scene 5. The Flight. The happy reunion is marked by rolling chords first on the harpsichord then on the harp-lute, framing phrases of quiet intensity for solo violin and viola. The couple ride off towards France. Wishing them Godspeed in high-flown terms, the Boy is rebuked for affectation by Master Peter and angrily corrected by Quixote when he refers to the city quaking with the noise of bells sounding the alarm for Melisendra's escape ('quasi campane' on the horns). 'Among Moors there is no ringing of bells but beating of drums and squealing hautboys.' Master Peter sticks up for the boy, reminding Don Quixote that plays are full of absurdities.

Scene 6. The Pursuit. When the Boy describes, and Quixote sees, the Moors in pursuit of the Christian pair (here horn and xylophone prominently if mysteriously quote the 'Canción del fuego fatuo' from *El amor brujo*), the old man's chivalrous feelings boil over. Convinced that the illusion is reality he advances on the tiny stage and lays about him with his sword. Master Peter laments the destruction of his puppets – and his livelihood. Don Quixote declares himself as 'knight errant and captive of the most fair and peerless Dulcinea', to whom he sings a short prayer before addressing the public on the virtues of knight-errantry, 'above all the professions that are in all the wide world'. The scene is punctuated by repetitions of a two-bar phrase in semi-quavers, usually preceded by an accented chord of G major, from a Catalan Christmas song 'El Desembre congelat'. With Quixote's interruption and the switch of interest to him, Falla brings the work on to a new plane without losing touch with what has gone before.

The sources of the music of the *Puppet Show* were numerous and various. The spur was the invitation from the Princesse de Polignac to write an opera for her private puppet theatre in Paris. Falla's childhood passion for toy theatres and puppets was reawakened in Granada by Lorca, who shared it. One Twelfth Night entertainment they devised embraced *Las habladores* of Cervantes, a mystery play about the Three Kings and a piece by Lorca which has not survived. Enrique Franco states that the instruments used were harpsichord, lute, violin and clarinet, and that Falla based the music he arranged for it on old Spanish sources including the Catalan carol later used in the finale of the *Puppet Show*.

Many years earlier, Falla had attended two lectures given in Madrid by the critic Cecilio de Roda on the musical aspects of *Don Quixote*, to mark the tercentenary of the book. Roda used as his main sources (summarised by Demarquez in her biography) a guitar manual by Gaspar Sanz (d. 1710) and the treatise *De musica libri septum* published by Francisco de Salinas in 1575. To these Falla, for his opera, added the *Cancionero* of his master Pedrell. There were of course more recent influences in the form of contemporary works for small ensembles which would now be described as 'music theatre' – *Pierrot lunaire*, *The Soldier's Tale* and perhaps one other work by Stravinsky, *Renard*. The last-named was also a Polignac commission, written earlier but not performed until the year (1922) in which the *Puppet Show* was completed. One of the remarkable features of the work is the writing for the Boy (called in Spanish *trujamán*, for which 'narrator' is a better translation than the literal 'interpreter'). For his narrations, which he delivers by rote in high-pitched monotone with the emphasis sometimes falling on the wrong syllable, Falla made a study not only of plainsong but of the street-cries of Andalusia with their traditional cadences and inflections (Ex. 16).

Ex.16 Master Peter's Puppet Show

-fe - ros a su es - po - sa Me - li - sen - dra, que es - ta - ba cau - ti - va en Es - pa - ña, en po - der de mo - ros, en la clu dad de San - sue ña.

In spite of the scoldings he receives from Master Peter and Don Quixote the Boy becomes steadily more involved in the drama, a fact Falla underlines by gradually incorporating his part, at first unaccompanied, into the instrumental texture. By the end of the fourth scene, when the Boy describes the reunion of Gayferos and Melisendra, the process is complete. The voice part is still confined mainly to one note but the manner of delivery is now different:

Ex.17 Master Peter's Puppet Show

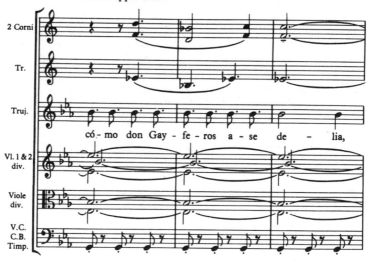

The *Puppet Show* is perhaps the foremost example of Falla's method of synthesis, fusing national, historical and popular elements into a whole which, in spite of the profusion of components, appears fresh and wholly spontaneous. The scoring (for flute/piccolo, 2 oboes, cor anglais, clarinet, bassoon, 2 horns, 2 trumpets, timpani, percussion, harpsichord, harp-lute or pedal harp, and strings) is masterly over a wide range of expression from extreme delicacy (Melisendra's music) through peasant roughness to knightly dignity. The scenes are tightly compressed but so adroitly contrasted that the work feels longer and bigger than it really is: the proportions are as finely calculated as those of Falla's garden at Granada.

PSYCHÉ

Voice, flute, harp, violin, viola, violoncello. Words by G. Jean-Aubry. First performance Barcelona, December 1924, by Concepción (Conchita) Badía. Published by J. & W. Chester, London, 1927.

Georges Jean-Aubry, a French writer on music, was a friend of Falla's from the time of the composer's first visit to France. He lived in England from 1915 to 1930, and edited *The Chesterian*, the house magazine of Falla's publishers, from 1919. The poem of *Psyché* is an elegant conceit in which the girl, the fatal lamp extinguished, is bidden to rise from her tear-stained couch and greet the golden noonday – birds are singing, the sun is smiling, Spring is stretching himself with a rose between his teeth. Falla, who liked visual as well as literary stimulus, however little the effect may have shown once musical considerations had taken over, prefaced the score with a mock-*Grand Siècle* inscription to Madame Alvar, the dedicatee, who introduced the song to Paris in 1925. In this inscription (presumably written for him by Jean-Aubry), he imagined as a setting for *Psyché* a court concert in the tower chamber in the Alhambra known as the Queen's Boudoir or Tocador de la Reina, during the visit to Granada in 1730 of Philip V of Spain with his Queen, Elisabeth Farnese.

The chamber-music scoring is similar, in the small number of instruments used, to the Concerto, on which Falla was engaged at the time, but it is entirely different in effect. The inclusion of flute and harp (as well as the words) gives *Psyché* a French atmosphere, but the slow saraband rhythm brings a hint of Spanish ceremonial. The voice part, with descending figures standing out above the silken rustle of the instruments, looks forward to the declamation of the *Soneto a Córdoba* and even to *Atlántida*.

CONCERTO

'Per clavicembalo (o pianoforte), flauto, oboe, clarinetto, violino e violon-cello.' (1) Allegro. (2) Lento. (3) Vivace. First performed Barcelona, 5 November 1926, by the Asociación de Música de Cámara, soloist Wanda Landowska, conductor Falla. Published by Max Eschig, Paris, 1928.

The description 'Concerto for harpsichord (or pianoforte)' is important. When Falla wrote the work, Landowska was almost alone in pioneering the revival of the harpsichord on an inter-national level. Though the concerto was conceived for the instru-ment, Falla knew that the choice would limit the probable number of performances. The piano was the approved alternative – at the first Paris performance in 1927 he himself played the work twice, once on each instrument. In a 'Note on performance' which follows the title-page of the score, Falla stresses the importance of a strong-toned harpsichord, 'aussi sonore que possible', placed well to the front of the other instruments. The expression marks for woodwind and strings should be 'regulated according to the strength of the harpsichord so as not to cover the sound, but they should of course observe the spirit and intentions of their markings'. He goes on to say that 'the harpsichordist, on the other hand, should increase all markings by one degree, while using for the greater part of the work the full sonority of the instrument'.

In a good performance (a mediocre one sounds scratchy) the sonority is not quite like anything else. It derives partly from Stravinsky's *Soldier's Tale* and other works of the same period, partly – in the composer's words – from 'ancient Spanish melodies, religious, court and folk tunes'. During a visit to Seville one Holy Week, Falla was much taken by the sound of oboes and bassoons in an early morning procession. The most striking theme of the first movement, however, is not Andalusian but Castilian, a song 'De los álamos vengo' by Juan Vasquez, from the *Orphenica lyra* of Fuenllana (1554). Pedrell included the song in his *Cancionero* as No. 71 of Vol. 3, referring in his introduction to a 'genuinely popular origin' (Ex. 18). In his programme note for the Barcelona première Falla quotes the tune as heard on its first appearance in the Concerto, without mentioning the origin.

Ex.18

De los a - la - mos ven - go ma -

- - dre

The three ascending notes with which the tune begins recur in slightly different form (the first step not a semitone but a tone) after the initial flourish at the opening of the slow movement. Since the finale was apparently written first it may be wiser not to make too much of a faintly discernible relationship between the leading theme of the finale with the toccata figure that opens the first movement. In any case the unity of the three short, concentrated movements depends more on balance, contrast and proportion than on thematic connections. The toccata figure which opens the work, oscillating between the keys of D and B, persists for twenty bars – quite a long time by the concise standards of this score – before the Castilian song, in Falla's version, is heard on flute and oboe (Ex. 19 overleaf). The harmony here as elsewhere in the Concerto looks and sounds bitonal, though Falla apparently insisted that the effect was the outcome of the principles of Louis Lucas, expounded in *L'Acoustique nouvelle*. The song comes twice more, the last time in augmentation on oboe, violin and cello. The final cadence of the movement repeats, forcefully, the jump from D to B.

The second movement, marked *giubiloso ed energico*, opens with rolling arpeggios for the harpsichord. Spread chords are a feature of the first movement: there are more now, sometimes arpeggiated inwards, moving in contrary motion, with grace-notes for extra sonority. Woodwind, squealing like organ reeds, and strings play close canons with a chant-like theme. There are rapid scales like pealing bells, an exhilarating crunch (Ex. 20, pp. 66–8) when the harpsichord rolls out the chant in C against flailing chords in E for the other instruments, and at letter 7, during one of the soloist's rare silences, some sudden pianissimo chords for the instrumental body like a distant tolling.

The movement, which begins in A and ends in F sharp, resembles a solemn but passionate sacred dance. It is dated at the end *A. Dom. MCMXXVI. In Festo Corporis Christi*. The finale, marked *flessibile*,

Ex.19 Concerto

scherzando, is Scarlattian not in the pastiche sense but in the full one of rhythmic vitality and adventurousness (note the independence of the cello part). In place of spread chords there are trills and mordents.

When, as sometimes happens, it is performed coolly and non-committally, the Concerto turns dry and elusive. It was evidently not so in the composer's hands. Ann Livermore noted that before the slow movement Falla 'bent his head, closed his eyes and folded his hands in sign of prayer'. Others have noted that after he had played the work at an ISCM Festival at Siena, the keyboard was spotted with blood from his fingers. The recording he made (on a Pleyel harpsichord) about the time of the Paris première is revealing for steady tempi and splendidly vital rhythms, the slow movement filled with physical as well as spiritual intensity.

Ex. 19 (cont.)

The Barcelona première, with the dedicatee Landowska as soloist, was apparently tentative and under-rehearsed. However, the statement that Landowska did not play the work again is incorrect. According to Denise Restout, assisted by Robert Hawkins (*Landowska on music*, London 1965) she gave several performances in American cities, including New York, Boston and Philadelphia.

SONETO A CÓRDOBA (SONNET TO CORDOVA)

Voice and harp (or piano). Words by Luis de Góngora. First performed Paris, 14 May 1927, by Magdeleine Greslé and Mme Wurmser-Delcourt (harp). Published by J. & W. Chester, London, 1956 (originally Oxford University Press, London, 1932).

Ex.20 Concerto

The tercentenary in 1927 of the death of Góngora, 'father of the baroque poetry of Europe' as Trend called him, was marked by celebrations, for which the guiding spirits were a number of Spanish poets of what became known as the '27 generation. Among them were Gerardo Diego, Rafael Alberti, and Lorca. One task was to persuade their eminent friend Falla to set some verses of a poet of whom he took the conventional view that his style was frigid and precious. They were successful. Falla's choice fell on the Sonnet to Cordova, Góngora's native city, written at Granada in 1585. In the sonnet the poet praises the walls, towers and great river of his birthplace, the fertile plains and lofty mountains round about it, mighty with pens as well as swords. If, at Granada, among the ruins

Ex. 20 (cont.)

and spoils watered by the two streams, he should forget Cordova, he will never again deserve to see his homeland, the flower of Spain.

Writing during the composer's lifetime, Trend said: 'Directness has always been a passion with Falla.' He set the sonnet for voice and harp (or piano) in sturdy yet flexible declamation of an almost disconcerting directness. The voice part has something of Quixote's solo in the *Puppet Show* and something of the Narrator in *Atlántida*. Those are for low, male voices. The Sonnet is usually sung by a soprano. As Trend observes, she needs 'the attributes of a baroque angel'. If only his writer friends had persuaded Don Manuel either to set a sequence of sonnets or to choose a longer poem! Now the disadvantages of Falla's increasingly meagre output become apparent. The Sonnet lasts just over two minutes. Not many singers will engage a harpist for such a short piece. Although the piano is an adequate substitute (Falla himself used one for a record-

Ex. 20 (cont.)

ing of the song), the unusual original instrumentation has surely contributed to the neglect of a vigorous and typical work.

BALADA DE MALLORCA (BALLAD OF MAJORCA)

Mixed unaccompanied choir. Words by Jacint Verdaguer. First performance Majorca, Monastery of Valldemosa, 21 May 1933, by the Capella clássica de Mallorca. Published by Ricordi, Milan, 1975.

On behalf of the Chopin Committee which organised annual commemoration of the winter (1838–9) Chopin had spent on the island with George Sand, and of the Capella clássica which he conducted, the indefatigable Fr Juan María Thomas had asked in vain for permission to perform part of *Fuego fatuo* and even *Atlántida*. Falla was courteous but firm. As a recompense he gave the choir a short new work of four minutes duration. The compliment was as finely turned as the music. The *Balada de Mallorca* is a version for unaccompanied voices of the *andantino* section of Chopin's Ballade No. 2 in F, Op. 38, written on the island. Falla took his text from the tenth canto of Verdaguer's *L'Atlàntida*. The words (not used in Falla's *Atlántida*) have a likeness to the Polish poem by Mickiewicz from which, so Schumann says, Chopin drew the inspiration for the F major Ballade. Verdaguer describes the mythical origins of the Balearic islands: a girl filling her pitcher from a spring near the shore drops the vessel, which rolls into the sea and breaks into three pieces. The ocean, grieving for her, turns the pieces into islands golden with roses. With only slight departures from Chopin's scheme – some 'la-ras', wordless 'oh' and 'ah' vowels and *bocca chiusa* sounds, and the addition of a few brief but telling phrases for the sopranos (Ex. 21 overleaf) – Falla has set the music so naturally on the voices that the pianistic origins are forgotten. In his book *Manuel de Falla en la isla* Fr Thomas, who presumably had access to a manuscript, states that Falla changed Chopin's tempo marking *andantino* to *andante sostenuto*. In the Ricordi edition, however, the marking is *andantino tranquillo*.

HOMENAJE (HOMAGE)
'Le Tombeau de Claude Debussy'

Guitar solo. First performed (on harp-lute) Paris, 24 January 1921, by Marie-Louise Casadesus. First performance on guitar, Paris, 2 December 1922, by Emilio Pujol. Included in 'Le Tombeau de Claude Debussy', supplement to the special number of *La Revue Musicale*, Paris, December 1920. Published separately by J. & W. Chester, London, 1921.

In spite of the influence the guitar had on his earlier music, especially on his writing for the keyboard, Falla had written nothing for the instrument except a few phrases of on-stage accompaniment in the wedding scene of *La vida breve*. The Catalan guitarist Miguel Llobet, a pupil of Tarrega, had been pressing him for a work when a meeting in Paris with Henry Prunières, editor of *La Revue Musicale*, led to a request for an article for the special issue Prunières was preparing to commemorate Debussy, who had died in 1918. Falla wrote the article (reprinted in *Escritos sobre música y músicos* and in the English version *On Music and Musicians*) and, with Llobet's request in mind, also wrote a guitar piece for the musical supplement, 'Le

Ex.21 Balada de Mallorca

Tombeau de Claude Debussy'; the other contributors to this supplement were Bartók, Dukas, Goossens, Malipiero, Ravel, Roussel, Satie, Schmitt, and Stravinsky.

Falla's memorial to the composer he so much admired is a dark elegy, marked *mesto e calmo*, soberly exploiting the guitar's potential for chords, rapid scales, arpeggios, and variety of weight, colour and accent on single notes. There is a recurring refrain on two notes a semitone apart (though the effect is different, the interval is the same as the opening theme of the *Noches*), the purest conceivable small-interval figure within the degrees of the chromatic scale and also, surely, a reference to 'La Sérénade interrompue' (from the first book of Preludes), which Falla insisted on counting among Debussy's Spanish pieces:

Ex.22

(a) Falla, 'Le Tombeau de Debussy'

(b) Debussy, 'La Sérénade interrompue'

The *Homenaje* is a combination of references to Debussy's now permanently interrupted serenade to the Andalusia he knew only at second hand, yet sensed so accurately. There are allusions to *Ibéria* and at the end a phrase, twice heard, from 'La Soirée dans Grenade' (*Estampes*). The habanera rhythm used by Falla is common to both 'La Soirée dans Grenade' and to 'La Puerta del Vino' from the second book of Preludes. The sensual ache of *Ibéria*, which Falla reflected so potently in the first movement and epilogue of the *Noches*, is absent here. Instead, there are bare skeletons. Falla made his own transcription for piano, and subsequently orchestrated the piece as the second movement of the suite *Homenajes*.

Pour le Tombeau de Paul Dukas

Piano solo. Details of first performance in this form not known. Included in 'Le Tombeau de Paul Dukas', supplement to the special number of *La Revue Musical*, Paris, May–June 1936. Published separately by Ricordi, Milan, 1974.

Although on the surface Falla's music may reveal more of the influence of Debussy and Ravel, of all the famous musicians whom he met in Paris before the Great War it was conceivably Dukas to whom he owed the most. Dukas introduced him to Debussy and to Albéniz. He guided Falla's studies in orchestration and took the initiative over the production of *La vida breve*. The example of the notoriously self-critical Dukas may have sharpened Falla's natural fastidiousness and helped to form his habit of slow, careful preparation. As a man Dukas was friendly and, outwardly at least, uncomplicated; perhaps less alarming to the shy Spanish visitor than were some of the other Parisian luminaries.

Dukas died in 1935. By the end of the year, Falla had finished the short but eloquent page he contributed to this other 'Tombeau' published by *La Revue Musicale*. His fellow mourners on this occasion were Tony Aubin, Elsa Barraine, Julien Krein, Olivier Messiaen, Gabriel Pierné, Joaquín Rodrigo, Guy Ropartz and Florent Schmitt. Falla's tribute is a solemn, march-like procession of big chords, never rising above the initial *forte ma dolce*. There is a certain similarity to the opening of *Atlántida*, and more to the first movement of the Piano Sonata of Dukas. This work was obviously in Falla's mind: seven bars before the end of his tribute he quotes, in the transitional form Dukas gives it before using it as a fugue subject, the theme of the trio of the Sonata's scherzo. The result is so unlike anything Falla had previously published that the neglect of the piece by pianists, though regrettable, is understandable. As with the Debussy elegy, the effect in a good performance is out of proportion to the modest dimensions of the music. In Falla's own orchestration, the piece became the third movement of the orchestral suite *Homenajes*.

HOMENAJES

For orchestra. (1) Fanfare, sobre el nome de E. F. Arbós, (2) à Cl. Debussy (Elegia de la guitara), (3) à Paul Dukas (Spes vitae), (4) Pedrelliana. First performance of complete suite Buenos Aires, 18 November 1939, conductor Falla. Published by Ricordi, Milan, 1953.

Falla's last completed work, the suite *Homenajes* (Tributes), is a composite score covering the years 1920 to 1938. Only the fourth movement, *Pedrelliana*, was new. The 'Fanfare on the name of E. F. Arbós' was written for the seventieth birthday of the distinguished violinist and conductor, long active in the service of contemporary Spanish music. The letters of his name, using Ré (D) for R, Do (C) for O, Sol (G) for S, served fourteen composers including Falla as material for short celebratory pieces performed under the direction of Arbós at a concert in Madrid on 28 March 1934. Falla added the initials of the subject's Christian names, E(nriques) F(ernández). He scored his fanfare for horns, trumpets and drums. The sound has a bracing, open-air quality that makes a sudden likeness at letter 4 to Janáček's Sinfonietta seem appropriate. The second and third numbers of the suite are orchestral versions by Falla of the Debussy and Dukas tributes discussed above (Falla, so meticulous about notes, was sometimes inconsistent about titles). The scoring of the Debussy elegy stresses the drained, funereal atmosphere of the guitar original. The Dukas one (the words 'Spes vitae' (Hope of Life) were added to the title) is more sonorous. The contrapuntal foundation of the processional chords comes out more clearly on the orchestra but in neither of these two movements is the orchestration a positive gain. The Debussy and Dukas tributes are separated in the suite by a short nine-bar recall of the Fanfare.

'Pedrelliana', a tribute to the revered master who had died in 1922, is a different matter. This is the longest movement of the suite. Falla made it out of themes from the opera *La Celestina*, published in vocal score but, though Casals performed excerpts at his concerts in Barcelona, still not produced on the stage. It was like Falla to draw attention to the beauties of a neglected major work. This opera is based on the play of the same title by Fernando de Rojas (1475–1541), and the protagonist is a bawd; in view of Falla's scruples about the possible bad influence of his own stage works, one wonders if this choice did not involve some searchings of conscience.

As with *Psyché*, Falla used as point of departure an imaginary scene, nothing to do with the opera but (according to Pahissa) a pastoral landscape in the style of the frescoes in the Campo Santo at Pisa – ladies seated in the shade, singing and playing instruments while the menfolk hunt. Falla subdues his own personality to his master's – even a cursory examination of *Los Pirineos* and *La*

Celestina proves that Pedrell had a distinct tone of voice. The first section is mostly concerned with the sounds of the hunt. After an unexpectedly passionate climax there comes a series of delightful tunes, presumably of ancient origin, suggesting that one after another the court ladies rise to dance or sing. The tunes are repeated and intermingled. The opening horn-call is heard again, and for the last few bars the hunt music takes over. The mood of pastoral relaxation is curiously like the *Siegfried Idyll*. In an entirely different way the score is as unexpected as the Dukas elegy. It must have disconcerted those admirers of Falla who were still expecting 'Andalusian' music of the kind he had stopped writing years before. That is no longer important. *Pedrelliana*, which is quite conceivable as a separate item, deserves to be heard more often.

The suite *Homenajes* is scored for triple woodwind, 4 horns, 3 trumpets, 3 trombones, tuba, timpani, percussion, celesta, harp, strings.

MISCELLANEOUS WORKS

Fanfare pour une fête (Fanfare for a Festival), Falla's tribute (there were other fanfares by Bantock, Goossens and Satie) to a new music periodical, which survived for seven issues, was a fanfare thirteen bars long, for two trumpets, timpani and side drum, in which the trumpets are employed contrapuntally, with some sturdy cross-rhythm. Falla later used the top line as the theme of the 'Games of the Pleiades' section of *Atlántida*. Later still, Halffter decided to use the fanfare itself at the beginning of the previous section of the work, 'The Gardens of the Hesperides'.[1]

Falla was attracted to the 'autos sacramentales' or sacred dramas of Calderón. Through his friend Sert he received but did not accept an invitation from the theatrical producer Max Reinhardt to write music for a Calderón play to be given at the Salzburg Festival. Falla annotated his copy of two plays with similar subjects, *Los encantos de la culpa* and *Circe*, but the pull of *Atlántida* proved stronger. Not long afterwards, for friends in Granada, he wrote and adapted music (from the *Cantigas* of Alfonso X and the *Cancionero* of Pedrell) for *El gran teatro del mundo* in 1927, and in 1935 did the same for

[1] Published in the first number (October 1921) of the fortnightly review *Fanfare* (Goodwin and Tabb, London). Reproduced, with an article by Laurence Ager, in the *Musical Times* of November 1967.

Lope de Vega's comedy *La vuelta de Egipto*.

A curiosity of the period is an arrangement for solo piano of the *Canto de los remeros de la Volga* (Song of the Volga boatmen), written in 1922 and first performed in Granada in 1971 by Manuel Carra. A dissonant, percussive, sonorous, wholly unexpected treatment of the familiar tune, presumably written for some occasion now forgotten.[1]

Unpublished choral works written during the years at Granada include a minute but striking *Invocatio ad Individuam Trinitatem* for three unaccompanied voices with a fourth voice added for the Amen, lasting barely over a minute but demonstrating Falla's absorption in the polyphonic style. The *Invocatio* was written and performed at Granada in 1928. For the Capella clássica of Majorca (which performed it in 1934) Falla arranged an excerpt from the *Amfiparnaso* of Orazio Vecchi. His interest in polyphonic music also led him to make some 'versiones expresivas' of various motets etc. by Encina, Escobar, Guerrero, Morales and Victoria. Two of the Victoria arrangements, *Sanctus* and *Ave Maria*, were sung under Falla's direction in Spain, others of the 'versiones' were included in the second of the Buenos Aires concerts of 1939. In the *Ave Maria*, the original note values in the lines 'Sancta Maria, mater Dei, ora pro nobis' are lengthened for emphasis. Such editorial liberties might be thought out of place now, but Falla's versions sprang from a desire to communicate to others the profound emotion contained in this music – especially, as he explained to Mossèn Thomas, the director of the choir in question, in such details as these notes, 'large, round and open like rose windows blazing with light'. Falla's approach, however, was not the late-romantic one of making old music acceptable to the public of the day by dressing it up and filling it out. He preferred to hear his favourite, Victoria, performed by a small number of singers. 'Four unadorned voices', he maintained, enabled certain passages to 'move the deepest fibres of the soul with incomparably greater force than an orchestra of a hundred instruments.' Don Manuel's authenticity was of the spirit rather than of the letter.

A *Himno marcial* for male voices in unison arranged from the 'Canto de los Almogávares' in the third act of Pedrell's *Los Pirineos*, with new words by José María Pemán, has been mentioned.

[1] Published by Unión Musical Española (Madrid, 1980) in vol. 3 of *Obras desconocidas*.

Like other eminent musicians from Europe, at the beginning of the Second World War Falla found himself in the Americas. His case was not as drastic as those of Bartók, Schoenberg or Stravinsky. He was not, strictly speaking, an exile. No one had forced him to leave Spain. He could have gone back there, if he had wished to and been physically strong enough. In a letter to Segismundo Romero dated 26 May 1941, he wrote of his and his sister's desire to return after 'the terrible cloud of war' had passed. There were difficulties, however. He was too frail to return more than twice to Buenos Aires to conduct concerts for Radio 'El mundo'; two a year, he had calculated, would suffice for his financial needs. Modest these needs may have been, but little or nothing was coming in. Falla's royalties, frozen during the Civil War, were now (his principal publishers being in London) blocked by the Second World War. Finally, the Spanish Society of Authors offered him a monthly allowance on account. But when he received an unexpected windfall from a film company in the USA (for granting them permission to film Rubinstein playing the 'Ritual Fire Dance'), he waived further payments from Madrid until other exiled Spanish musicians could be granted the same kind of help.

Alta Gracia was chosen, not for cultural amenity, but for peacefulness and a kindly climate. Falla did not lack company. The conductor, Erich Kleiber, was a neighbour. There were musical visitors (some of whom had come like himself to Argentina from Spain) such as the singer Conchita Badía and Falla's future biographer Jaime Pahissa. What was lacking was the kind of professional assistance that might have helped to bring order into the chaos still prevailing in some of the unfinished parts of *Atlántida*. Towards the end he met and took a liking to a young Argentinian musician, Sergio de Castro, who did some copying for him and proved sympathetic company, but their acquaintance did not begin until the year before Falla's death. (Castro subsequently went to Paris and became a painter.)

In a last letter to Romero, Falla listed the ailments and afflictions of the Argentinian years – an operation, exhausting haemorrhages, 'interminable-seeming fevers', an attack of iritis which affected his sight for six months . . . (The exact nature and cause of Falla's illnesses and the extent to which they may have been psychosomatic have still to be investigated.) As his health declined, hypochondria increased. He spent hours each day on minute care of his person (he had always, however conventionally and severely he dressed, been particular about his appearance). He adopted an extreme form of Spanish hours, with lunch at three or four in the afternoon and dinner at midnight. The domestic problems this created, Argentinian staff not being accustomed to such a régime, no doubt drew on even María del Carmen's store of saintly patience. Yet he remained 'a great talker', still capable of being his old, hospitable, companionable self. When the conversation interested him he would be carried away, forgetting for the moment his medicines, his chronic fear of draughts, or the walking-stick he was now accustomed to use. When he could, he worked on *Atlántida*. One half suspects that the unfinished task had become a necessary prop of his existence. There was in Falla a streak of credulity, and a strange vulnerability to superstition, unexpected in a man of his intelligence and strong faith. His fear of the baleful influence of the full moon was a relic of the time of *El amor brujo* and gipsy frequentations. He was convinced that his own life was divided into seven-year spans (this was partly true) and that his departure from Spain in 1939 marked the beginning of a new phase. On the morning of 14 November 1946, a few days before his seventieth birthday, he was found dead in his room after a heart attack. The funeral took place at Córdoba in Argentina. The embalmed body was taken by sea back across the Atlantic to Cadiz, his birthplace, where he was buried in the cathedral crypt.

ATLÁNTIDA

Scenic cantata in a prologue and three acts (unfinished, completed by Ernesto Halffter). Text adapted by Falla from the poem by Jacint Verdaguer. First concert performance (excerpts only) Barcelona, 24 November 1961, by various choirs, Victoria de los Angeles, Raimundo Torres and the Barcelona City Orchestra, conductor Eduardo Toldrá. First stage performance Milan (Teatro alla Scala), 18 June 1962, conductor Thomas Schippers. Published (first version) by Ricordi, Milan, 1962.

The idea of *Atlántida* came to Falla in 1926 after reading newspaper reports of celebrations for the fiftieth anniversary of the completion of the poem *L'Atlàntida* by the Catalan priest-poet Jacint Verdaguer. The dedication of the poem was dated a few days before Falla's birth – the kind of coincidence that appealed to him. The

77

project was discussed with his friend and supporter from Barcelona, Juan Gisbert Padró, during a railway journey to Zurich for the ISCM Festival. On return to Spain, Padró sent Falla a copy of the poem. With typical thoroughness, he was then asked to find a Catalan dictionary of the time of Verdaguer (1845–1902). Though Falla set the Catalan text, he called his work *Atlántida*, dropping the definite article and the Catalan accentuation from Verdaguer's title.

In a note written for the EMI recording, Halffter states that Falla began work on the score on 29 December 1928. By then he had given a newspaper interview about his plans and discussed them with friends including the painter José María Sert, who was to be responsible for the decorative side. Falla had also made pilgrimages to the southern part of Andalusia, to his birthplace Cadiz and to neighbouring sites traditionally connected with Hercules and historically with Columbus – the first category included the lonely, blanched and silent hill-town of Medina Sidonia, where there is a niche in a house-front with a small and venerable figure of the demi-god.[1] The mood of cautious optimism about *Atlántida* changed as prudence and a natural bent for secretiveness led Falla to be chary of news of such progress as there was. He was distracted by the necessity for travelling inside and outside Spain, for writing occasional works, less important but more urgent. His health began to deteriorate and so, during the next decade, did the internal political situation. He began to realise that he must use more of the poem than he had meant to, widening the scope of his work beyond the dimensions originally envisaged. Difficulties arose over the text itself, difficulties not concerned with the subject or quality of Verdaguer's poem but with its suitability for music, especially for dramatic music. During the 1930s *Atlántida* appears to have limped along. Writing to Juan María Thomas in 1935, Falla observed that he had reverted to 'the old snail's pace'. Three years later he was lamenting to the same correspondent his inability to finish 'this poor *Atlántida*, ever calling to me with great cries'. By that time the Civil War had isolated him at Granada. His last years in Argentina were

[1] When Falla was in Cadiz again in 1930 some friends took him to the off-shore islet of Sancti-Petri, where there is a view of the Atlantic stretching into the western distance. They reminded him of an old tale that when the sun sets in that sea the disc of fire can be heard sizzling as it strikes the water. Falla watched alone. When they asked him, 'Did you hear the sun hiss, Don Manuel?' he replied, 'No, but I heard many other things.'

equally, if for different reasons, solitary. Only if Falla's notes over the whole of this long period are published will the exact stages of composition become clear (meanwhile a useful outline will be found in Enrique Franco's essay 'La grande avventura di *Atlántida*' in the June–October 1962 number of *Musica d'oggi*).

The subject of Verdaguer's poem embraces the myth of the drowned continent of Atlantis and the exploits in the Peninsula of the demi-god Alcides (otherwise Herakles or Hercules) as well as the historical voyage of Columbus across the Atlantic and the carrying of the Catholic faith to the Americas. Falla made his own adaptation, adding some lines in Castilian from various sources for the 'Salve en el mar' and a few more in Latin – these include Seneca's prophecy. Since the final choice of text for the second part had not been made when Falla died, words for the 'Jocs de les Pleiades' (Games of the Pleiades) were supplied by José María de Sagarra. The following brief synopsis differs in some respects from the 1962 version.

Prologue: 'L'Atlántida submergida' (Atlantis beneath the waves). A tempest at sea, with a ship sinking. The 'corifeo' (narrator) appears, carrying a boy rescued from shipwreck. The boy is the future Christopher Columbus. The narrator tells him of the drowned continent and of the garden of the Hesperides. Who will save Spain, moored like a gondola on the raging sea? The answer comes with the 'Hymnus hispanicus' (Spanish hymn) – the Almighty will save Spain. The chorus sing of the land's future greatness.

Part 1: 'L'Incendi dels Pirineus' (The burning of the Pyrenees). The narrator, whose subsequent contributions are not specified in this synopsis, describes the journeys of Alcides from the banks of the Rhone to Spain, where the Pyrenees are aflame. Alcides rescues the queen, Pyrene. She tells how, last of a royal line, she has been driven to the northernmost borders of her realm by the monster Geryon who has seized her lands, cattle and sceptre, and fired the forests. With her dying breath Pyrene implores Alcides to avenge her. The hero destroys the wasted mountains and sets up a new range in her memory. He then descends to the sea-coast to board a waiting boat ('barcino') to sail in search of Geryon. The chorus sing the 'Cantic a Barcelona' (Canticle to Barcelona) in honour of the city that will occupy the site.

Part 2: 'Alcides i Gerió tricèfal' (Alcides and the three-headed

Geryon). Alcides lands at Cadiz and confronts the cringing and deceitful monster (sung by two tenors and a baritone), who directs his attention westward to Atlantis. The hero is granted a vision of the fair land ('Cantic a l'Atlàntida' – Canticle to Atlantis) and resumes his journey. 'L'Hort de les Hesperides' (The gardens of the Hesperides) and 'Els jocs de les Pleiades' (The games of the Pleiades). The seven Pleiades, daughters of King Atlas, are playing round the sacred orange tree. They sense that Alcides is the hero destined to overcome the Atlantid giants. Geryon has not told Alcides of the dragon with tongues of fire hidden in the topmost branches of the sacred tree, but the hero kills the venomous beast. The Pleiades mourn for the dragon and themselves expire. Out of pity they are translated to the heavens as a constellation. 'Arribada d'Alcides a Gades' (Arrival of Alcides at Cadiz). Alcides returns to Cadiz and plants a sprig from the orange tree as a pledge to future fertility. Beside it there springs up a dragon tree weeping tears of blood. 'Veus messatgers' (Messenger voices) and 'La veu divina' (The voice of God). At this point, the God of the Old Testament intervenes. Atlantis, luxurious and presumptuous, is bidden to go on her knees and mend her wicked ways. Alcides, having glimpsed the face of Jehovah, sunders with his club the mountains joining Spain to Africa. The waters rush through the gap. 'L'enfonsament' (The flooding). Atlantis is engulfed. 'L'Arcàngel' (The Archangel): the voice of an archangel announces that the catastrophe is God's punishment. 'Non plus ultra': Alcides erects a pillar on either side of the new straits and with his club inscribes the words 'Non plus ultra' – No further!

Part 3: 'El pelegrí' (The pilgrim). Columbus, seen briefly as a boy in the Prologue, is now a grown man, musing near the Pillars of Hercules. He hears distant voices intoning Seneca's prophecy that the known boundaries of the world will be pushed well beyond the limits imposed by the mythical hero. More voices identify Columbus as the man who will do this. They direct him to Isabella of Castile. 'El somni d'Isabel' (Isabella's dream). In her palace at Granada, Isabella the Catholic embroiders a mantle while her ladies and pages dance a galliard. The queen has dreamed of a dove (*columba*) flying over the sea with a precious ring in her beak, dropping it in the waters, from which arise flowery islands. Isabella gives her jewels for the construction of new ships. King Ferdinand and Queen Isabella are seen in a vision, as the chorus repeat God's command to the mariner to 'bring together my sons and daughters from the ends of the earth'. 'Les caravelles' (The caravels). Three ships appear, carrying the sons of the provinces of Spain across the waters. The chorus parts recall the 'Hymnus hispanicus' in the Prologue. 'La salve en el mar' ('Hail Mary' on the high seas). Columbus at prayer, surrounded by his sailors. 'La nit suprema' (The final night). Columbus watches alone on deck on the night before landfall. The chorus extol the 'Dies sanctificatus' or Holy Day about to dawn. (This condensed synopsis does not include the titles of every section, some of them quite short, of the text.)

As the description 'scenic cantata' and the sequence of events imply, some kind of symbolic staging or visual accompaniment was envisaged. Whether Falla was clear or consistent in his own mind about what he wanted remains unproven: in any case it is not surprising that over the long years of composition his views should have altered. The prime mover on the decorative side was Sert. It is clear from his correspondence with Falla (excerpts are included in the recording leaflet referred to above) that at least up to 1939 Sert was still devising ways and means of staging *Atlántida*, even if 'staging' was to be interpreted in the widest sense. Until he left Spain, at least, Falla wanted the first performance to be given in or near Barcelona (in a monastery like Poblet, for example) by the Orfeó Català choir. Even before the days of mixed media the dividing lines between opera and oratorio had become blurred. Perhaps significantly, a pioneer work in this direction was (or might have been if it had won any circulation) Pedrell's 'festival lirico popular' *El Comte Arnau* of 1904. But most of the works of the mixed-genre type to which *Atlántida* belongs came about a quarter of a century later. Obvious examples are Stravinsky's 'opera-oratorio' *Oedipus Rex* (1927), Milhaud's *Christophe Colomb* (1930), which made use of film, and on a more popular level Orff's *Carmina burana* (1937), another 'scenic cantata'.[1] Falla, for his part, was mov-

[1] When Falla discovered that Milhaud was working on a similar subject the two composers exchanged letters. It became clear that there would be no serious overlap between Falla's text based on Verdaguer and Milhaud's by Claudel. Milhaud thereupon dedicated his opera to Falla, who accepted gratefully while regretting he could not return the compliment, since his own dedication, to four great Spanish cities, had been determined. There is a certain piquancy in this interchange of friendly courtesies between the least prolific and the most prolific of the major composers of the first half of the 20th century.

ing away from the theatre. After Sert's death in 1945, he wrote to a friend: 'Now I am only concerned with the music, without thinking of the production . . . I am working on it day by day, but how little time there seems to be!' His own death was only a few months away.

The autographs of *Atlántida* passed to Falla's brother, Germán. When the decision to complete the work had been taken, they were entrusted to Falla's younger colleague, Ernesto Halffter, a friend and disciple since the days of the Orquesta Bética. On examination Halffter found that the state of the material was briefly as follows:

Prologue: Complete, composed and orchestrated by Falla except for a few bars of the 'Hymnus hispanicus'.

Part 1: Composed by Falla, orchestration largely lacking.

Part 2: The least complete, most confused part of the score, with sketches and alternative versions to be sorted out and pieced together.

Part 3: In a fairly advanced stage of completion, some parts orchestrated, some joins to be made.

Halffter was faced with something more daunting than the tasks confronting Alfano with Puccini's *Turandot*, Jarnach with Busoni's *Doktor Faust*, or more recently Cerha with Berg's *Lulu*. The world of music had to wait until 1961 to hear even part of *Atlántida* – the Barcelona première consisted not of the complete reconstruction, but of large excerpts. There followed stagings of the work at La Scala in Milan, in Berlin and Buenos Aires, and a concert performance (large excerpts again) at the Edinburgh Festival. Halffter however withdrew the score for consideration. Night descended once more over *Atlántida* until 1976, the centenary of Falla's birth, when what was described as the definitive version was heard in concert form at the Lucerne Festival. Part 2 was considerably shortened and the work now ended after 'La nit suprema', that is to say, before the moment of discovery. Again Halffter withdrew the score, this time only for a matter of months. An augmented 'definitive version', with some of the excisions in Part 2 restored, was given at the Granada Festival of 1977 – this is the version recorded by EMI.

Of the various difficulties that beset Falla, already briefly described, the least considerable must have been the necessity for writing other works. Even for a composer who approached the smallest task in a spirit of minute thoroughness, the minor things written after 1927 (all of them now to be seen as offshoots from the stem of *Atlántida*) cannot be considered as major distractions. The decline in his health and in the political situation of Spain were more serious. Most serious of all, because it could have affected the whole form of the work, may have been an increasing awareness of the disadvantages of his text. The desire, in view of his mother's descent and the support and friendliness he had met with in Barcelona, to write a Catalan work, is understandable. So is the appeal of Verdaguer's subject, uniting myth and history connected with cities and regions of Spain especially dear to Falla in a fervently Christian setting. Theatrical effect was none of Verdaguer's business. None the less, in spite of the intensely dramatic events with which his colourful epic is concerned, the lack of dramatic interplay between individual characters, hardly less necessary for an oratorio than for an opera, would have proved a handicap to any composer. Pyrene and Isabella have one monologue each. Columbus sings one phrase as a boy. As man he is mute. So is Alcides, to whom most of the strenuous action falls.

The main trouble came with Part 2, incoherent in the nature of the cataclysmic events described, and in addition containing Verdaguer's fusion of pagan myth with Christian interpretation. Here Falla was unable before he died to reduce the scenario, let alone the music, to definite and tractable form. The appropriate solution, however unacceptable to a progressive composer in the 1920s and '30s, would have been a symphonic poem for orchestra on the lines of Bax's *Garden of Fand* or *The Oceanides* of Sibelius, on a Straussian scale. In the Prologue and in Parts 1 and 3 Falla could build large structures out of concise, tightly-packed sections of his normal, modest but apposite proportions. Part 2 demanded something different. One wonders if the wish for secrecy prevented this literate man from consulting literary friends such as Lorca, whose experience as a dramatist might have been useful whether or not he liked Verdaguer's poem. Since the last part of *Atlántida* to be completed was apparently Pyrene's noble monologue in Part 1, the cause of incompletion was evidently not failing powers of invention.

Atlántida is not and cannot be the complete masterpiece lovers of Falla's music were hoping for, yet even in an incomplete state it forms a worthy culmination to a life utterly and selflessly devoted to music. Some kind of symbolic staging in a great church is con-

Ex.23 Atlántida, 'Canticle to Barcelona'

ceivable; even without this staging a church would be a more sympathetic and fitting location than a modern concert hall. For audiences unfamiliar with the subject-matter static illustrations painted (or more likely projected) on screens or wall might be helpful, though the danger with this kind of treatment is that strong designs may be a distraction, merely adequate ones may add nothing, poor ones may distract in a different way. On the whole, not only on account of the quality of the choral music but because

Ex. 23 (cont.)

in a concert hall the difficulty of following the action described in the text is lessened, *Atlántida* should probably be seen primarily as a gain to the choral repertory. The long, enforced absence of the score from concert programmes may be one reason why little has been said about the excellence of Falla's vocal writing both for solo voice and for chorus, shown in greater variety and quantity in *Atlántida* than in the shorter works.[1] Typical examples of the choral writing are the sinewy counterpoint of the 'Burning of the Pyrenees' and 'Canticle to Barcelona' in Part 1 (Ex. 23, pp. 84–7)

[1] The 1962 vocal score of *Atlántida* distinguished for stage purposes between 'action' and 'narration' choruses. In the concert hall, though the chorus may be divided, the distinction becomes unimportant. A similar division occurs in Pedrell's *Comte Arnau*.

Ex. 23 (cont.)

and the serenely devotional polyphony of the last two sections of the whole work; of the solo writing the sad, Monteverdian lament of Pyrene, the radiant romance of Isabella and, perhaps most characteristically, the gruff, measured declamation for the narrator (Ex. 24, pp. 88–9), a grown-up, sobered-down equivalent of the enthusiastic boy 'trujamán' in the *Puppet Show*. The narrator's part is one aspect of *Atlántida* that shows traces of Pedrell's *Los Pirineos*, for example the writing for the Bard in the Prologue to that opera.

In Part 2 Halffter (one must agree with Enrique Franco that for his work in this part alone Halffter should rank as joint-composer of *Atlántida*) has partly reverted to musical language of a richness

Ex. 23 (cont.)

Falla had abandoned, and also made use of choral and orchestral effects which at first seem out of keeping with the general austerity. Yet the text justifies, indeed virtually compels, such a decision. The juicy modulations of the 'Canticle to Atlántida' (deployed at more generous length than Falla usually allowed himself) and the 'Games of the Pleiades', in which Flower-maidens from *Parsifal* sport in Debussy's sea, provide the necessary contrast of atmosphere with the more severe outer parts. The more highly-coloured effects in the later episodes of this part are a reminder that we do not know how Falla would have handled a large orchestra after the time of *The Three-Cornered Hat*. As for vocal effects, it must be said that the use

Ex.24 Atlántida, 'Burning of the Pyrenees'

CORIFEO *pesante molto con forza*

En - tant, vo - ra el Ro - se, a
Or pres - so al Ro - se, de -

Poco meno lento *vibrante*

simile sempre

8va bassa

l'hé - roe a-pe - dre-guen de - for - mes i ra-bas-suts ge -
- for - mi gi - gan - ti s'at ten - tan a la pi - dar l'e -

loco

- gants mes quan creu en a Al - ci - des en - tre
- ro - e, ma quan-do ai ra - mi ap - peso Al - ci - de

Ex. 24 (cont.)

Ex.25 Atlántida, Alcides returns to Cadiz

of choral speech in the 'Voice of God' section comes as an anti-climax. On the other hand, Part 2 contains one of the loveliest passages in the work, the simple, intimate chorus, a dozen bars long, known by Spanish musicians as the 'Madrigal to Cadiz' (Ex. 25 above and overleaf). It comes when Alcides, resting awhile from adventure, returns to the 'daughter of the waves, palace of mother-of-pearl and ivory'. Into the texture Falla weaves two brief, tender references to the Pantomime in *El amor brujo*.

Falla's temperament and his piecemeal method of composing over a long period of time made it unlikely that *Atlántida* would break new ground in the way Stravinsky often did during those same years – though Falla's debt to Stravinsky, in the punchy

Ex. 25 (cont.)

ostinatos of the 'Hymnus hispanicus' and in the striking bell-figure
(Ex. 26) in Part 2, is still evident. Falla was not a musical explorer
of the same unremitting, outward-looking curiosity. At least by the
later years of the period devoted to *Atlántida*, he was more concerned with spiritual than stylistic progress. Further development
along the lines of the Concerto, a short work for a few instruments
designed for performance under chamber-music conditions, was
hardly to be expected in what emerged as a full-scale work for large
forces intended for large, popular audiences. In spite of the composite nature, *Atlántida* gives an impression of strong musical
personality. In his note for the Edinburgh Festival performance of
1962, Martin Cooper described the style as 'a wholly personal

Ex. 25 (cont.)

Ex.26 Atlántida, part two
Lento

language capable of both austere dignity and sensuous expressiveness'. Some aspects of this style, like the grafting of the Spanish musical past on to Falla's idiom, were foreseeable. Others come as a surprise – the opening bars (Ex. 27), a concentrated impression of

Ex.27 Atlántida, Prologue
(Visione del mare in tempesta con un vascello semi affondato)

the ocean heaving over submerged Atlantis, ambiguous and dis-
quieting as a fragment of primitive sculpture; the candid, fresh,
subtly-metred strains of Isabella's dream (a symbolic inter-weaving
of two folksongs, one from Granada, the other Catalan – Ex. 28
overleaf); the profound solemnity of the 'Salve en el mar' and of the
final page of the work, where Bach seems to be holding watch with
Victoria and Pedrell. Falla sometimes spoke of his ambition to write
a Mass and 'prayed that the moment would arrive when he could
realise his wish worthily and with the necessary serenity of mind'.
That moment never came, but the more inward parts of *Atlántida*
give an idea of what might have been.

The dedication is: 'To Cadiz, my native city, to Barcelona, Sevilla
and Granada, to which I also owe a debt of profound gratitude.'

Ex.28 Atlántida, Isabella's Dream

ISABEL

ISABELLA

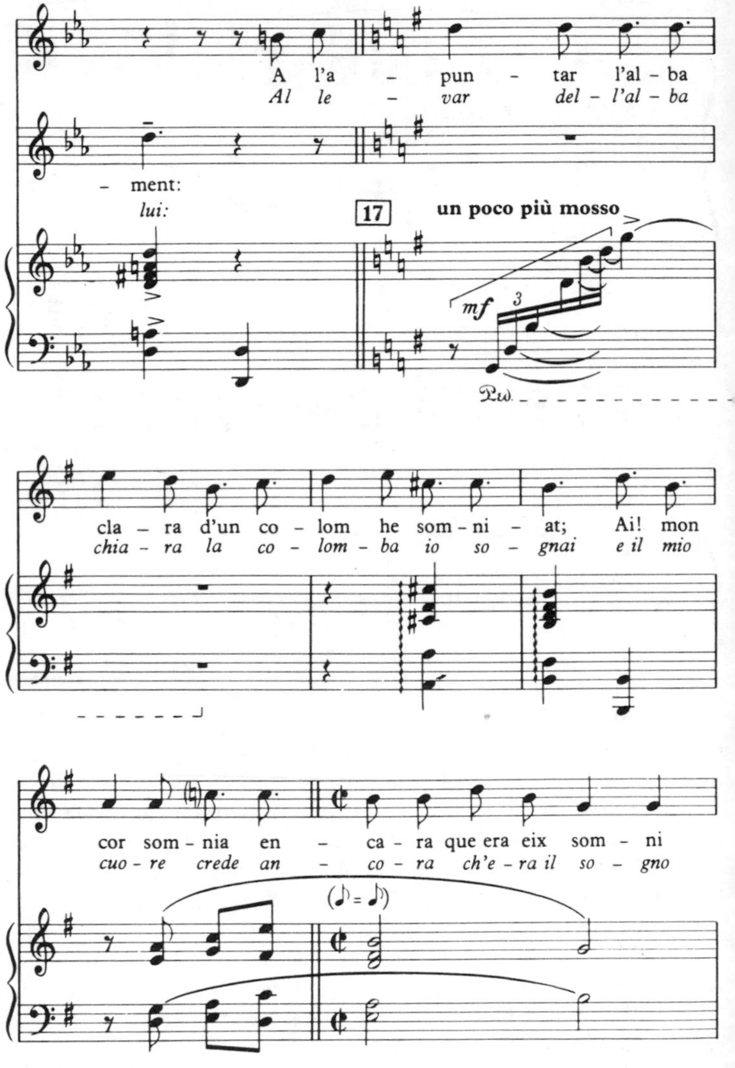

Ex.28 (cont.)

The orchestra consists of triple woodwind, 4 horns, 4 trumpets, 3 trombones, 3 tubas, a large array of percussion, 2 harps, 2 pianos, strings.

Style and Man

Attitudes to Falla's music have changed during the past few years, not among those who remain faithful to a handful of works (or excerpts from works) but among musicians who formerly more or less ignored him. 'Manuel de Falla,' wrote the Italian critic Fedele d'Amico in 1962, 'is one of those composers whom everyone calls great but whose name, when the music of this century is discussed, almost everyone forgets.' The oversight is attributed by d'Amico to the inferiority complex afflicting leading propagators of a very exclusive concept of 'modern music' into which Falla's music, among others, declines to fit. Recently, however, Boulez recorded two works, and Berio orchestrated the *Seven Spanish Folksongs*. Renewal of interest came from various sources, from the reassessment of Debussy and Ravel, from the return of picturesque titles (titles have more influence than people realise: Falla only wrote one major work with an abstract label). Largely, renewed interest came from new attitudes to Spain and a new régime in that country – Spain has probably changed as much since Falla's departure as it had during the long, slow centuries between the Golden Age and Falla's lifetime. Generations have grown up which did not experience the Civil War. Spain has become at least superficially familiar to thousands of tourists. General Franco, whose lengthy rule started about the time Falla left Spain, is dead. Folksong, at least in the guise of 'ethnic music', is no longer a dirty word.

Similarities have been suggested between the condition of music in Spain and in Britain at the beginning of this century – and at the beginning of Falla's career. But as far as he was concerned there was greater similarity between two countries at the opposite ends of Europe, Spain and Russia. Pedrell put Spanish music on the map in theory while his former pupils, Albéniz and Granados, were putting it there in practice. To these three Falla stands roughly as Stravinsky to Rimsky-Korsakov and the composers who followed after the major Russian nationalists. The analogy is not exact. Falla had more admiration for Albéniz and Granados (and learned more from the former) than Stravinsky for, say, Glazunov. Both Falla and Stravinsky came near the tail end of their respective countries' nationalist movements (Russia and Spain have exceptionally long tails, wagging fitfully to this day), both underwent pronounced evolutions of style. Stravinsky's, through his enquiring, inquisitive and acquisitive nature, was much the more radical.

Falla reached maturity as a composer during the First World War, when reaction against post-Wagnerian music and the unwieldy, uneconomic apparatus of Mahler, Strauss and Skryabin was under way. Paris helped Falla to become a better Spanish composer and also ensured that he became, and remained, a European one. Fortunately Falla's inclinations and the roles history chose him to play usually coincided. He was by instinct a concise composer with a horror of superfluous notes: he learned to write intensely Spanish music which was not copious (*Iberia* and *Goyescas*, the piano works which crowned the respective careers of Albéniz and Granados, are prolix in their generosity); in the case of Pedrell the scale, also generous, of *Los Pirineos* and *La Celestina* does not encourage compression. In spite of his devotion to Pedrell, Falla differed from him on one important point. Pedrell favoured direct use of 'the document', not only quoting traditional tunes in their original form but sections of old music. Falla preferred a different approach. 'In all honesty', he wrote in an essay dated 1917, 'I think that in popular song the *spirit* is more important than the *letter*. The essential features of these songs are rhythm, tonality and melodic intervals. The people themselves prove this by their infinite variations on the purely melodic lines of the songs . . .'

cf. Gustav Mahler, 96
but not Strauss.

Searching for the spirit he found the essence, which marked him in various ways, in the harmonies produced by the tuning of the guitar strings, which had fascinated composers well before his day – not only Glinka, but Domenico Scarlatti – and in the themes or figures contained within small intervals typical of Andalusian (and not only Andalusian) folk music, the kind of tag-phrases that men and women hum half-consciously as they work.

Writers on Falla attach some importance to the book *L'Acoustique nouvelle* by Louis Lucas, which Falla picked up second-hand in Madrid. Lucas (1818–?1865) was an obscure French polymath who also published books about medicine and chemistry. According to the *Biographie universelle des musiciens* of Fétis (2nd edition, Paris 1863) the title of the original edition (Paris 1849) of the book by Lucas was *Une Révolution dans la musique. Essai d'application à la Musique d'une théorie philosophique*. The poet Banville contributed a preface. Fétis alleges that the book 'did not sell three copies' and that the remainder of the first printing was reissued in 1854 under a new title as *L'Acoustique nouvelle. Essai d'application* etc., with a new title-page bearing the legend 'deuxième édition'. Though his entry on Lucas will give pleasure to those who enjoy academic malice, Fétis should be taken with a grain of salt. He resented what he considered plagiarisms from his own writings, not mentioned by Lucas. *L'Acoustique nouvelle* is concerned with acoustics only in the broader sense. It is mainly a harmony treatise with knobs on, the knobs being discussions of topics advanced for the time but of interest to musicians of Falla's generation and later. Lucas questions the supremacy in Western music of the semitone as the usual subdivision of the tone. He refers with admiration and interest to music of other civilisations – for example, Greek, Indian and Arab. He recommends the study of bird songs and animal cries and mentions Molière's ambition to devise notation for correct theatrical declamation. He praises Monteverdi. There is less than commentators have implied about 'natural resonance' and the harmonic series, but much about enharmonic intervals. One footnote likely to appeal to Falla cites the untutored singing of young Breton peasant girls as an example of 'the harmonic genus in all its purity. The theme uses such a small number of essential notes that they can often be contained within a single tetrachord. But they are laden with embellishments and above all with enharmonic modifications and inflections . . .'

Falla told Roland-Manuel that without Lucas his music would not have developed as it did. From the little book he evolved his technique of 'internal rhythm' – 'the *harmony* in the deepest sense of the word born of the dynamic equilibrium between the periods. The virtue of this equilibrium lies in the spacing of cadences and consequently of the judicious placing of tonal centres.' Roland-Manuel, presumably still paraphrasing Falla, further defines internal rhythm as 'supposing a synthesis between rhythm in the normal sense and a tonality founded on natural resonance'. Poulenc, more simply, referred to it as 'secret architecture'. One might perhaps extend the term to cover the outward sense of proportion for which, with the partial exception of *Nights in the Gardens of Spain* and the *Fantasía baetica*, Falla's mature completed works are so remarkable. Since he is a more systematic composer than is generally realised, a detailed study of the degree to which the theories of Lucas acted as guide or stimulus would be welcome, though it lies outside the scope of this book and the powers of the writer. One must hope for the eventual publication of Falla's annotations to his copy: Roland-Manuel apart, his professions of indebtedness are not exactly documented.

Meanwhile a hint may be gleaned from Falla's essay on Wagner of 1933 (trans. David Urman and J. M. Thomson):

It is necessary to be fully convinced of the fundamental truth offered by the natural acoustic scale in order to establish the harmonic – and therefore contrapuntal – basis of the music, as well as to give a tonal structure to a series of melodic periods which, being generated by the same resonances which integrate that scale, have to move at different levels. What I mean is that the intervals forming that column of sounds are the only real possibility for the constitution of the chord, as well as an infallible norm for the tonal-melodic construction of those periods that, limited by cadential movements, compose every musical work.

(Unfortunately, the obscurity which Falla so successfully kept out of his music sometimes crept into his prose.) His use of 'vertical harmony' (roughly the sum of the essential notes of the melody), to be heard for example in *El amor brujo*, is one means through which he obtained unexpected sonorities from modest instrumental forces.

Another means was his profound feeling for orchestration, inborn obviously but sharpened by listening to and writing for small bands of varying capacity in Madrid theatres. Demarquez quotes a remark of this least boastful of composers to the critic

Henri Collet about the *Puppet Show* – 'You will see that I can make as much noise with twenty instruments as with a hundred.' Falla's preference for small orchestras and small choirs was in tune with post-First World War developments, but was as much a matter of conviction as fashion. He once confessed to Juan María Thomas that his dream was to have at his constant disposal a small choir and orchestra to try out his music for sound – the sort of facility that Pedrell, for one, had so notably lacked.

Once settled in Granada, when the spate of creative energy released by the return to Spain had grown smaller, Falla's rate of output declined as preparations for each new work grew more and more elaborate and the act of composition began to resemble an act of synthesis, the eventual result being the tip of an iceberg of meticulous research, trial and meditation during which the completion of a single chord was a milestone. Falla's small tally of published works (even when *Atlántida* is included) worries commentators. Perhaps they underrate the value of a series of compositions of however modest dimensions each with a definite individuality, worked to a high finish. One suspects the same critics might be no less ready to condemn other twentieth-century composers for writing too much. The pursuit of the happy mean is not a typically Spanish solution. However small the work in hand, Falla worked in depth. Each work is a new departure: he never repeated himself. The Debussy and Dukas 'homages', for example, have the gravity of classical slow movements or, say, a late Fauré Nocturne. The poet Valéry's words about Dukas in the commemorative number of the *Revue musicale* containing Falla's musical tribute are apposite:

I find in him [Dukas] what I have so much admired in certain other creative artists: a clear and clean rupture with any kind of facility. Those unable to conceive that infrequent production may be the result of an immense amount of preparatory work accuse such artists of sterility. I say to them that the innumerable rejections occurring during the labours of these lovers of perfection would suffice for the fame of many artists less strict with themselves.

Falla remained firmly within the bounds of tonality. Writing in 1916 he referred to Schoenberg's atonality as 'this extremely grave mistake', a remark which found echoes through many decades in countries less musically isolated than Spain. Falla himself was not isolated except in his later years. At least up to the time of the Civil

War he remained in touch with developments in Europe, attending ISCM Festivals and befriending a large number of musicians from other countries. Falla belonged consciously but not dogmatically to the Latin civilisation: to him the gulf between himself and Schoenberg must have seemed unbridgeable, though Pedrell's last pupil, Roberto Gerhard (an acquaintance of Falla's in Barcelona), studied with Schoenberg during the twenties (he left Spain the same year as Falla). If he had lived a few years longer, Falla would have seen the chasm crossed again, in the direction of Schoenberg by Dallapiccola and others, in that of Webern by his old friend, Stravinsky. The suggestion of Burnett James[1] that 'in the search for brevity, concision and absolute purity' Falla and Webern were at least moving in the same direction has some justification, unlikely as it may have seemed at the ISCM Siena Festival in 1928, when Webern's String Trio, played immediately before the *Puppet Show*, caused a riot. As a consequence of his interest in polyphonic church music and folksong he made much use of modes, not applying them externally as decorative colour but using them organically as part and parcel of the fabric and thought. In spite of his French affiliations he did not often employ the whole-tone scale. One exception is *Atlántida*, where the occasional whole-tone flavour (at the beginning and in the Hesperides music in part two) seems to be associated with the exotic nature of the doomed continent.

Considering the time at which he lived and the amount of prejudice he must have encountered in Paris, Falla remained coolheaded and objective about Wagner. His direct experience of German-speaking lands was minimal: his preference for hearing Wagner in the concert hall rather than the opera house may have been due to never seeing a good performance. He had deep respect, reflected in more than one page of *Atlántida*, for *Parsifal*. Juan María Thomas found him one day on Mallorca seated at the piano, with a vocal score elaborately marked with coloured pencils, making a detailed analysis, explaining that 'so long as it was done with humility and good faith, it was a useful exercise'.

Stravinsky's observation in *Memories and Commentaries* that Falla's nature 'was the most unpityingly religious I have ever known – and the least sensible to manifestations of humour' is familiar. The description fixes one facet of that nature much as Picasso's oftenreproduced drawing of 1920 fixes Falla's features in a mask of

[1] In *Manuel de Falla and the Spanish Musical Renaissance* (London, 1979).

melancholy, uncomfortable submission (compare the drawing, made in the same year, of Satie seated in what appears to be the same chair, winking connivingly). Though Zuloaga was a much lesser artist than Picasso his portrait of Falla penetrates the mask, revealing more of the sitter's character. Similarly, though Poulenc was a lesser composer than Stravinsky, his description of Falla in *Moi et mes amis*[1] is more widely perceptive and more generous. Poulenc's remarks about Falla's mysticism have been quoted. On a mundane level Poulenc noted his behaviour at rehearsal: 'He never lost his temper but became nervous and restive, with a kind of Spanish irritability familiar to me from my teacher, the pianist Ricardo Viñes. With both these men, conversation would suddenly take on the tone of a guitar, furiously preluding.'

Where his faith was concerned, Falla's sense of the ridiculous does indeed appear to have been tenuous. José María Pemán and other writers tell how, when the composer was discussing with an impresario a possible performance of *Atlántida* (when ready) in the ruined monastery of Poblet near Barcelona, he explained that the 'Voice of God' in Part 2 would be sung by children, since only they were fitted for the task, adding that naturally at that moment the whole chorus would sink to their knees. Thinking no doubt of the tiered seating normally provided for choruses on concert platforms, the impresario demurred. With 'the holy rage that sometimes overcame his natural courtesy' Falla held his clenched fist before the impresario's face as he enquired, 'But how can one not fall on one's knees if one hears the Voice of God?' When Pemán was asked to fit words to the Pedrell tune Falla had adapted for the *Martial Hymn* there ensued several meetings in Granada followed by an exchange of letters – even this minor and unwelcome chore was undertaken with typical thoroughness. In one of his letters Falla asked Pemán if he did not think that in a certain line the word 'bayonet' came too near the word 'God'. At least, when he was unhumorous, Falla was drily so.

He was such a strange, endearing (and no doubt occasionally maddening) man, such a bundle of deeply-held beliefs, inconsistencies and fads that there is a temptation to drift into too much anecdote, forgetting that the personal eccentricities were the outward manifestation of inner tensions of much greater significance. These tensions arose largely from the opposition in his nature

[1] Interviews with S. Audel (Paris–Geneva, 1963).

between the monk-like, celibate side which became stronger as he grew older, and the other side which could with such certainty capture the alternating joy and despair in popular music and paint feminine portraits as warm and distinct as those of Salud, Candelas and the Miller's Wife, to which may be added the more circumscribed but no less definite Melisendra, Pyrene and Isabella.

Some of the best writing about Falla came in the double number (4–5, July–October 1962) of *Musica d'oggi* published by Ricordi in connection with the production of *Atlántida* at La Scala. Massimo Mila makes the interesting suggestion that 'Isabella's Dream' is modelled on the 'typical *romance* of nineteenth-century lyric opera' and instances in particular Marguerite's 'Chanson du Roi de Thulé' in Gounod's *Faust* (in melodic curve if not in general treatment there is a stronger resemblance to the corresponding 'chanson gothique' in the *Damnation de Faust* of Berlioz). Whether or not there is any connection the possibility illustrates Falla's synthetic methods of composing, the symbolic fusion of Andalusian and Catalan tunes with an archaic-style accompaniment (Falla's re-creations avoid the impression of pastiche), fusing in turn with a possible influence from nineteenth-century opera, finally emerging as a chastely radiant lyrical scene shot through and through with Falla's individuality. Mila further suggests that *Atlántida* became for Falla 'a kind of creative rethinking of the history of music ... not unlike the one systematically undertaken by Stravinsky in his neo-classical phase'.

That is not quite how Stravinskyan neo-classicism or *Atlántida* strike us nearly two decades later: now we are more conscious of the composers than their models. The two composers' attitudes were quite different, Stravinsky testing himself against the past, voraciously absorbing it, Falla rather seeming to wish to be absorbed. For that matter their 'pasts' were different, Stravinsky approaching his selected periods as an outsider, scrutinising them objectively, Falla's Spanish past (which to some extent still existed) not strange but home. In another essay (quoted at the beginning of this section) from the same issue of *Musica d'oggi*, Fedele d'Amico goes to the heart of the matter when he defines the 'miracle of Falla, probably unique in our century: that the simplicity, the irreproachable grace, should be the outcome of the most thoughtful elaboration ...' With Falla style and man are very close, but the man always adds something. D'Amico continues: 'Probably the key to the